The imperial controversy
challenging the empire apologists

Andrew Murray

D1313124

manifesto

First published in 2009 by Manifesto Press

Manifesto Press
Ruskin House
23 Coombe Road
Croydon CRO 1BD
info@manifestopress.org.uk
www.manifestopress.org.uk

Cover
Dervishes at the battle of Omdurman
A contemporary image of the revolt against British colonial rule
in the Sudan

Typset in Bodoni
Printed in Britain by North Wolds Printers Ltd

ISBN 978-1-907464-00-3

Contents

for Anna

Foreword

Now it is not good
For the Christian's health
To hustle the Aryan brown,
For the Christian riles
And the Aryan smiles
And he weareth the Christian down;
And the end of the fight
Is tombstone white
With the name of the late deceased,
And the epitaph drear,
'A fool lies here
Who tried to hustle the East.'

Rudyard Kipling

EVEN as notorious an advocate of Empire as Kipling could sense the writing on the wall in 1891, the very the point when the European carve-up of the globe reached its apogee. He, of course, had the benefit of ruminating on two failed British occupations of Afghanistan – the first resulting in arguably the greatest military disaster in British history. That didn't prevent a further bloody adventure in 1919. Now we are engaged in a fourth.

The perversion of political life that has attended the renewed imperial posturing of the last eight years is matched only by the shameless rewriting of the history of Empire, which remains a nightmare from which the British national psyche struggles to awake. Andrew Murray's Imperial Controversy provides the requisite bucket of cold water. The timing of this broadside could not be better, nor the quarter it's launched from: since the inception of the Stop the War movement in September 2001 the author has been at the centre of the great political battle against empire which this book is a contribution to. That engagement lifts this book above so many others that have tried to account for the catastrophic course George Bush and Tony Blair embarked us upon, before they headed off to the lucrative global lecture circuit.

It is easy now, but still necessary, to indict that gruesome pair. Indeed, many of those who share their guilt are busy doing just that while hoping the rest of us quietly forget their own role. Murray, however, hones in on the cadre of intellectual adjutants who provided the justifications and obfuscations for what is now rebranded "the long war". Some of them are still at it, inflicting their cod social psychology and even worse history on the people of Afghanistan, Somalia and Iran. The peerless diarist of the Nazi era, Victor Klemperer, was shockingly direct in his verdict on those who played an analogous role in Hitler's Germany:

"If one day the situation were reversed and the fate of the vanquished lay in my hands, then I would let all the ordinary folk go and even some of the leaders, who might perhaps after all have had honourable intentions and not known what they were doing. But I would have all the intellectuals strung up, and the professors three feet higher than the rest; they would be left hanging from the lamposts for as long as was compatible with hygiene."

An extreme reaction, certainly, but one which has the virtue of stripping away the hypocrisy of those whose breathless op-ed pieces and endlessly promoted Boy's Own histories have paved the way for others to go to their deaths.

These self-styled pro-war liberals will no doubt find the above allusion to the Nazis' crimes a symptom of what they claim is the "moral relativism" of those of us who oppose Empire. In so doing, however, they reveal the sleight-of-hand of the new imperialists, which has been to relativise the crimes of European and latterly American empire, through flattering comparison with the barbarity of Nazism.

Murray's scrupulously sourced account of the murder and mayhem unleashed by European colonial expansion corrects the picture. It is a history that was never told at the time in the West, but seared into the memories of the East. Never losing sight of the specificity of the Nazi regime, he shows how the ideology of genocidal racism, the practice of mass, state-directed slaughter, the modern technology of killing, the apologetics of lawyers and professors, and the depravity of occupation were all trailed, tried and tested in Africa, Asia and the Americas – before the poison was sucked back into Europe and spewed out by fascism.

As he notes, the corporate book chains are full of works on every aspect of the Third Reich, and no offensive against one or other Third World state is complete without a reference to a "Mussolini on the Nile", "Islamo-fascism" or "the new Hitler". But airbrushed out or worse is the bloody story of Amritsar and Congo, not to mention the never-named Afghan villages destroyed by drones piloted from spick and span control rooms in Europe or America.

Imperial Controversy allows today's wannabe imperialists to damn themselves out of their own mouths in the same way as any account faithful to the record must do of their forebears. Each prior travesty has an idiotic contemporary counterpart. Lord Curzon of India to Nick Cohen of Euston (does anyone remember that epoch-making Manifesto drawn up on the back of a beer mat?) – if ever there was a case of first time tragedy, second time farce, that is one.

It hasn't taken the decades of the British Empire for the pronouncements of the B52-liberals to be put to the test. That has come rapidly and rudely. After the Iraq disaster, half way through the river of blood in Afghanistan, and with the two leaders most responsible defenestrated – though not from great enough a height – it beggars belief that the pro-war *literati* are still churning out the same garbage. But they are. And, more importantly, the imperial impulse remains. If anything, it is likely to increase as corporate capitalism tries to dig its way out of the economic quicksand it's stumbled into.

All of which makes this book so important. Those who think themselves familiar with the subject matter will nevertheless find new gems and clarity of presentation. Newer readers will find more than an introduction, based on an unshakable commitment to equality between nations and opposing all forms of racism. Both will benefit from the mordant arguments it develops and which have stood up to a thousand interviews and hostile commentators.

And therein lies the great merit of Imperial Controversy. With no complacency, it exudes confidence that the battle against the new empire is being won. Murder in the guise of a civilising mission continues. But more and more people are turning against the reality of these wars. This book will help them understand where those wars, and the racist delusions they depend on, come from – and how to end them once and for all.

George Galloway MP
London, August 2009

Introduction

Considering Tony Blair's foreign policy in 2005, John Lloyd, a leading journalistic supporter of the invasion of Iraq, sent a prayer heavenwards, declaring that he expected British foreign policy to stay neo-conservative after the premier left office. "Blair was the path-breaker. Let us hope that the path he broke remains the one trodden by his successors." [1]

In the short-term at least, it is clear that Lloyd is destined to be disappointed. The Iraq War has tested public support for what he described as neo-conservatism's "coupling of national security with the promotion of freedom," well past the point of destruction. Gordon Brown has withdrawn the last British troops from the south of that devastated country, bringing to an end, if only for reasons of electoral expediency, an inglorious and unpopular passage in British military and diplomatic history. And in the USA, Barack Obama is signalling at the very least a different approach and rhetoric. While the full implications of the new administration remain to be worked through, it does not seem that it can be reduced to a continuation of Lloyd's neo-conservatism. That episode is over, buried not just in the killing fields of Iraq, but in the collapse of neo-liberal economics at the end of 2008 and in the Russo-Georgian war of August that same year, all of which indicate the passing of the "unipolar moment" of unchallengeable US might – the moment of which neo-conservatism was a political expression.

But this beast is undead. The imperialist urge, rooted in the dynamics of the world economy (issues to be addressed in a further book in preparation), continues to cast a long shadow. Indeed, the economics of capitalist crisis has so often been the introduction to the politics of war. So the study of the ideological and political debates around the wars of the 21st century remains, alas, relevant.

This is not another book about the Iraq War, however. It is about some of the ideas and debates which have underpinned the "war on terror", specifically the attempt to rehabilitate Empire and imperialism as viable, even desirable, political projects. This incorporates a return to a rosy view of the history of the British Empire and a view that a renewed imperialism – or "interventionism" – can be placed in the service of human progress.

These debates are far from academic. They have helped frame and justify decisions which have led to perhaps a million deaths over the last eight years. Until they are rooted out of political life, the possibility that they will contribute to still worse disasters in future remains a real one.

This book aspires to arm those millions opposed to this policy with polemics and information. Its structure aims to follow the various arguments advanced in support of the Bush-Blair foreign policy. *Chapter One* examines the work of the explicitly pro-Empire historians, of whom Niall Ferguson is the best-known, and examines how it has been used to promote contemporary neo-conservative policy.

Chapter Two presents an alternative reading of the record of the British Empire, and of other colonial powers, the better to develop an understanding as to why the last thing the great majority of the world wants to see is a repetition, however dressed up. *Chapter Three* goes into greater detail concerning the history of imperial intervention in the Middle East in the hope of going some way towards explaining Arab and Muslim attitudes towards "the west."

Chapter Four locates the phenomenon of liberal interventionism in general, and Tony Blair's premiership in particular, in a history of argument within the progressive movement concerning imperialism. Finally, Chapter Five reviews the record and role of the "pro-war left" in relation to the Iraq War.

Chapter Three benefited considerably from work done by Dr Kate Hudson, of London South Bank University and chair of the Campaign for Nuclear Disarmament. Some of the material in Chapter Five has previously appeared in *The Guardian* and the *Morning Star*, or in *Stop the War: the story of Britain's biggest mass movement*, by the present author and Lindsey German. The whole has benefited from the comments of Seumas Milne of *The Guardian* and the design and editorial expertise of Nick Wright. None of them, of course, bears any responsibility for anything that appears here.

Andrew Murray

London May 5 2009

Chapter One
The rehabilitation of empire

"Britain has yet to come to terms with its imperial record. A fog of cultural amnesia about the country's recent colonial past pervades the debate about its role in the world today...there is precious little acknowledgement of the relentless and bloody repression that maintained a quarter of the world's population under British rule...of the hundreds of thousands who died in continual rebellions across five continents, or from forced labour and torture in prison camps...the ubiquitous racist segregation or deliberate destruction of economic prosperity in places like Bengal. The roots of the global crisis which erupted on September 11 lie in precisely these colonial experiences and the informal quasi-imperial system that succeeded them." – Seumas Milne, *The Guardian* [1]

"AMNESIA" ABOUT colonialism and its consequences has long been almost state policy in Britain, to the point of absurdity on occasion. The last book to be officially burned by the common hangman in the UK was an eighteenth century work by the Dean of Trinity College, Dublin, describing how British colonialism had reduced Ireland to desolation. The Secretary of State for India in the early 1900s was urged to ban the works of Macaulay within his domain lest the historian's very mild criticisms of Clive and Hastings alert the native public to the bloody and corrupt origins of the Raj. As World War Two drew to an end, it was easy to secure copies of Hitler's *Mein Kampf* in British-ruled India – but not any books from the anti-colonial All-India Progressive Writers Association, all of which were prohibited by the imperial censorship. [2]

More recently a cottage industry of apologias for imperialism has been allied to the official amnesia. If the Empire is not forgotten, it is because it is increasingly being celebrated instead. There is the possibly apocryphal tale of a Soviet historian warning Western colleagues that, in his country, "nothing is more dangerous than trying to predict the past". Nothing is safer, however, than rewriting history to suit the purposes of those presently in power. And that is what lies behind the contemporary offensive designed to cast a roseate glow over the colonial experience. History has been adjusted, tweaked, reinvented and sometimes just made up to suit the requirements of the renewed imperialism of official Washington and London.

At every step through the "long war" of the 21st century, conservative and neo-conservative politicians in the US and their "New Labour" counterparts in Britain have had their hands held by the ideological advocates of a renewed Empire – sometimes brazenly described as a new colonialism, more often enveloped in "democratic" justifications. Throughout, promoting a new Empire has meant whitewashing the record of empires past. Indeed, mobilising support – such as there has been – for the whole programme of "liberal" or "humanitarian" intervention has depended in part on persuading people that previous imperial policies were not so bad after all.

Criticism of imperialism is often derided as "politically correct," the catch-all damnation used by the political right against any progressive, liberal or sometimes merely polite point of view. The treatment of the subject in British schools remains either cursory or lop-sided, despite the large (and growing) number of pupils who trace their roots back to lands once in the grip of the Empire. A determination to avoid what conservative Australians resistant to confronting their country's extermination of its Aboriginal population call "black armband history" is now pervasive in Britain too. Indeed, eminent US historian Nicholas Dirks has noted that imperial history has been "written in the service of empire itself" and that "astonishingly, much imperial history is today still written as if the task of the historian is to achieve balance, and perspective, in the historical account of the costs and benefits of empire." He adds that the recently-published five-volume *Oxford History of the British Empire*, presumably set to become a definitive reference work for students of the subject, is written in exactly this spirit, ignoring criticisms of previous histories of Empire. "...despotism continues to be more acceptable when exercised in imperial contexts than in European ones, where the same kind of neutrality would be considered unseemly..." [3]

And as *Guardian* columnist Seumas Milne wrote in 2005: "The standard

GCSE modern world history textbook has chapter after chapter on the world wars, the Cold War, British and American life, Stalin's terror and the monstrosities of Nazism – but scarcely a word on the British and European empires which carved up most of the world between them and the horrors they perpetrated." [4]

And this is not just a matter of ignorance about history, which would be a vice but not a crime. Oxford historian Maria Misra asked the important question in 2002: "Does it matter that the British are smug about their imperial past, that British atrocities have been airbrushed from history?" Indeed it does, she pointed out: "a... worrying symptom of this rosy glossing of the imperial past is the re-emergence of a sort of sanitised advocacy of imperialism as a viable option in contemporary international relations." Misra errs only in seeing the contemporary advocacy of imperialism as being "sanitised." But she put her finger on the critical connection between a whitewashed past and a blood-soaked present. [5]

It is in the climate developed by the institutional "forgetfulness" or pre-meditated distortion of the real record of the old colonialism and imperialism that those looking to promote the new Empire started to do their work. The first toes were dipped in the water more or less as soon as the Berlin Wall came down and the perspective of a US-dominated world came fully into view, with Britain, of course, enjoying an honoured place in the sun.

The Pioneers

If any one ever believed that the collapse of the Soviet Union was going to lead to a world of peace and equality between nations they were not studying the *Wall Street Journal* with the required attention.

The main bully pulpit of aggressive US conservatism and the house newspaper of the American corporate elite was fast off the mark in seeking to revive the ideas of colonialism and Empire in the post-Cold War world. Every international incident in the 1990s appeared to provide material for the case for a return to the direct domination of the globe by the great powers – mainly, in fact almost exclusively, the USA.

Their initial intellectual inspiration was, however, not American at all, but the British historian and journalist Paul Johnson, who in the course of the

1970s and 1980s had migrated from a political position on the left of the Labour Party to being one of the most outspoken champions of Mrs Thatcher's premiership. His historical works bear the heavy imprint of his zealous conservatism, making them suitable texts for those in the "sole superpower" needing a bit of scholarly lustre to drape around their promotion of a *"US uber alles"* foreign policy.

Paul Gigot – as of 2009 the *Journal's* editor – turned to Johnson as early as 1992 in an editorial page feature article headed "Peace in Somalia may require new Colonialism". He drew the attention of his readers – the great and the aspirational of US big business – to an article by the historian in the *National Review* recommending that the United Nations Security Council "using one or more advanced powers as its agents" start "moving into the business of government, taking countries into its trusteeship for varying periods". This "is plainly needed in Somaliland now," Johnson wrote, using the colonial-era name for that unfortunate country, in case anyone still missed the point. [6]

Hoover Institution fellow Angelo Codevilla was next into the fray at the Journal with a piece insisting that it was "Time to rethink the Wisdom of Anti-Colonialism" – in this case promoting colonialism as the solution to the crisis then developing in the Balkans with the destruction of Yugoslavia. Codevilla was not coy about reaching for the rhetoric of racism, arguing that "nearly all post-Colonial rulers turned out to be **monsters** *(my emphasis)*, and decolonisation was a disaster." Having got this sweeping dehumanisation of, *inter alia*, Nehru, Nyerere, Nkrumah and Nujoma (that's just the 'Ns') off his chest, the Hoover scholar deplored the fact that "the US government has not begun to rethink the wisdom of anti-colonialism." He only required a bit of patience. [7]

A couple of weeks later, one of the newspaper's then-editorialists, David Brooks, took up the new party line calling for a "kinder, gentler colonialism." He wrote: "The second great contradiction of colonialism is that it is a marriage of power politics and moralistic impulses. In Britain, Fabian socialists such as George Bernard Shaw argued that if the Chinese government could not establish peaceful conditions for its people, then the Europeans should go in and do it for them.

"…if Americans do believe that all people are endowed by their creator with democratic rights and abilities, and if they are right, then a form of colonialism may be sustainable – one that goes into some of the places where authority has broken down and imposes order long enough to allow the locals to govern themselves. It would be a colonialism that restrains its moralising and improving impulses." [8]

These ideas were picked up – but not developed – by the then British Foreign Secretary Douglas Hurd, who told *The Independent* that the United Nations needed to take up an "imperial role". Denying that the great powers could themselves repeat the 19th century "scramble for Africa", Hurd argued that it therefore had to be the United Nations which took up the task, describing the UN in a revealing fashion: "The UN is us, the UN is the British, American and Russian taxpayer and the UN will need troops." Neither Hurd nor the Major government in which he served developed this point, but a marker had been set down.

In these early polemics, we can see traced out some of the issues which were later to arise far more sharply when the Johnson-*Journal* line of action became the settled policy of the George W. Bush administration in the US and the post-Major government, led by Tony Blair, in London.

First, the United Nations was in the early 1990s seen as an essential cover for any return to colonialism by the great powers, with the League of Nations "mandate" system as the template – which, among other things, assigned Palestine to Britain and Namibia to South Africa after World War One, thereby setting the stage for two bitter conflicts which rumbled on intractably – for seventy years in the latter case and to this day in the former. The moment for unabashed US unilateralism had not yet fully arrived.

Second, there was the coat-trailing for an alliance between US conservatism and the British "Fabian imperialist" tradition, located in imperialist social-democracy. George Bernard Shaw came to his senses with the passage of time; Tony Blair of course did not. The appeal to a pro-colonial tendency within British social democracy is far from being a total misreading of the latter's history, as we discuss later.

And finally, we can see the tension between colonialism as an exercise in power politics – what could be called the Cheney-Rumsfeld approach to the world – and those who wish to give the fullest possible rein to their "moralising and improving impulses," of whom Tony Blair and the authentic neo-conservatives in Washington like Paul Wolfowitz might be the exemplars, at least at their own valuation. The difference in practical policy may not amount to a great deal, but in terms of ideological rationale and propaganda justification, it is consequential.

With Clinton in the White House, the rhetoric of a new colonialism took a back seat, for the US government at least. The practice was, however, rather different. While Somalia was abandoned in some ignominy after the US marines turned out, unsurprisingly, to be unsuited for the "humanitarian intervention" which the President had set as their mission, two constituent parts of the former Yugoslavia, Bosnia and Kosovo, were brought under neo-colonial administration by the end of the century. And the guru of US neo-conservatism Irving Kristol wrote in 1997 that "without clearly intending it or fully realising it, the United States has come to dominate the world militarily and culturally. One of these days the American people are going to awaken to the fact that we have become an imperial nation." The moment of awakening – and of a government that did indeed clearly intend and fully realise its imperial destiny – was not far off. [9]

9/11 was the turning point. Paul Johnson was, unsurprisingly, first to raise the standard, with his platform of choice being, once more, the editorial page of the *Wall Street Journal* – the newspaper having been invigorated by the departure of the hated Clinton and the Supreme Court's appointment of George W Bush to take his place in the White House.

Johnson asserted that "the West may find that the only workable answer to terrorism is a new colonialism." He even helpfully supplied a list of states which "America and her allies may find themselves, temporarily at least, not just occupying with troops but administering..." These included Afghanistan, Iraq, Sudan, Libya, Iran and Syria. This should all be accomplished through a "'respectable' form of colonialism" like the mandate system of the League of Nations. [10]

Johnson and the *Journal* were no longer crying in an ideological wilderness. More sober voices joined in the cacophony. Martin Wolf, a senior *Financial Times* commentator, urged "the need for a new imperialism" demanding a "transformation in our approach to national sovereignty – the building block of today's world," joining Johnson in recommending "some form of United Nations temporary protectorate" for "failed states". [11]

It was at this moment that the inter-weaving of political support for Bush's "long war" with the revival of old historical narratives and stereotypes became more central. The eminent journalist and military historian Sir John Keegan, then the principal defence correspondent on the London *Daily Telegraph*, provided a particularly egregious example. Drawing deep at the well of traditional Empire prejudice and *Boy's Own* stereotypes he wrote that the war on terror "belongs within the much larger spectrum of a far older conflict between settled, creative, productive Westerners and predatory, destructive Orientals". He offered the Vietnamese as one of his examples of the "treacherous" way the "Orientals" conduct war – a people who, as Jonathan Mirsky observed in a rebuttal, were "heirs to over 2,000 years of Chinese civilisation – settled, productive." Moreover, they are a people who had comprehensively seen off two armies of "creative and productive Westerners", which no doubt is what really rankled with the Colonel Blimp at the *Telegraph*. [12]

But the post-9/11 development of most significance was the transition of Empire advocacy from journalism to government, from nostalgics and academics to ministers and top civil servants.

The first of the latter to put his head above the political parapet was again British, perhaps because in the USA open advocacy of Empire with a capital letter remains more politically difficult. At any event, if in the new empire it was the US doing the doing, it was the British doing the thinking, above all Robert Cooper, a senior Foreign Office official seconded to Downing Street as Tony Blair's foreign policy adviser (as of 2008 serving as a top EU foreign affairs functionary).

In a pamphlet published by the London think tank The Foreign Policy Centre early in 2002, to which Tony Blair supplied the foreword ("a timely contribution to the debate"), Cooper wrote: "Empire and imperialism are words that have become terms of abuse in the post-modern world. Today, there are no colonial powers willing to take on the job, even though the opportunities, perhaps even the need, for colonisation is as great as it ever was in the 19th century. What is needed is a new kind of imperialism, one acceptable to a world of human rights and cosmopolitan values." [13]

"A world in which the efficient and well-governed export stability and liberty seems eminently desirable.

"We already have voluntary imperialism of the global economy through institutions such as the IMF and the World Bank," Cooper added by way of an illuminating example. [14]

Cooper was, later, in the van of those having second thoughts: "Empire does not work today. A century of emancipation, of national liberation movements and self-determination cannot be reversed. Empire has become illegitimate," he wrote in October 2003. By then, however, the damage was very much done. [15]

Not everyone was so perceptive. US neo-conservative pundit Max Boot was still making the "case for wise liberal imperial rule" in the *Financial Times* in 2004. After the purely formal end of the US occupation of Iraq in the summer he wrote that it was "time to ponder the future of the American Empire", claiming that "there will continue to be strong demand for US interventions around the world," although he did not advise as to from whom this demand might come. Boot pressed the case for "liberal imperialism" to deal with world's troubles on the "Cromer, not the Curzon model", preferring the pragmatic approach of the British proconsul in Egypt who manipulated the government in Cairo while formally acknowledging Ottoman sovereignty, to the missionary zeal of Curzon, the Viceroy who directly ruled India on Britain's behalf. [16]

And former Murdoch-employed journalist Stephen Grey, reflecting on the disasters in Iraq, told the *New Statesman* readership they could be ameliorated by a yet more explicit imperialism. "Like it or not, Britain's mission in Iraq is neo-colonialist; it is about the projection of power and the installation of a new regime more acceptable than the previous one. For this job, we need people who serve not as soldiers but as administrators. It is time, then, to reinvent Britain's Colonial Office, with a staff of people who are prepared to rough it like the old political agents on the North-West Frontier...It could be called the Office for Foreign Administration or something like that. We need it. Look at the rush of interventions since the end of the Cold War – Bosnia, Kosovo, Sierra Leone, Afghanistan. Iraq is not a one-off." [17]

All these arguments depend on one thing above all – a distorted understanding of the real record of imperialism and colonialism first time around. That is where the new cadre of Empire-boosting professional historians come in – Andrew Roberts, Lawrence James and above all Niall Ferguson. All believe Empire was a good thing in the past and could be a better thing for the future. All, of course, supported the Iraq War.

The Historians

Would a creationist be asked to present a multi-part TV series on evolution? Only if it was explicitly billed as a controversial (albeit nonsensical) challenge to accepted science. Would a fascist sympathiser be given expansive airtime to make the case for Mussolini? Even in this time of rampant historical revisionism, it seems impossible.

Yet a historian who boasts of defending colonialism at the Oxford Union in his youth was given just that opportunity by Britain's Channel Four in 2003. The series propelled Niall Ferguson, scion of a family of white settlers in colonial Kenya, to the front ranks of the new breed of TV historians, from which eminence he has become a leading advocate of 21st century imperialism. [18]

This was a significant passage in the promotion of Empire. Robert Cooper and the *Wall Street Journal* speak mainly to a political and journalistic elite. Taking the message to a broader public, popularising the revival of the imperial mindset, requires television and the re-animation of prejudices and assumptions. Ferguson's first popular work, *Empire*, was concerned to rehabilitate the record of British colonialism while his second, *Colossus*, was an appeal to the US to take up the white man's burden (albeit with much fretting that it might not have the economic or political stamina to do so). His most recent, as of 2007, was *War of the World*, which aimed to put questions of nationality, race and ethnicity at the centre of an interpretation of twentieth-century history, at the expense of other social explanations.

He has not been alone in his work on this front. Andrew Roberts, perhaps most celebrated for his comprehensive biography of the quintessential

Victorian imperialist Prime Minister Lord Salisbury, has not been on the television as often as Ferguson. However, he has had the compensating distinction of being invited to dine at the White House with George Bush and Dick Cheney, so enamoured were the President and Vice-President of his subsequent (and much inferior) *A History of the English-Speaking Peoples since 1900*, and at Downing Street with Gordon Brown and Bush once more on the latter's farewell presidential visit to London in 2008. For a historian who describes himself as "very right-wing" these must have been special occasions, with any unpleasantness arising from Brown's party affiliation offset by his conviction, robustly shared by Roberts, that there is nothing to apologise for in the record of the British Empire. Roberts's book is an explicitly Churchillian attempt to re-cast the 20th century as one in which all good flowed from Britain and the USA and all the problems from everyone else. And there is Lawrence James, a writer of popular tomes on the Empire and the Raj who is not afraid to mix it with critics of the new pro-imperial orthodoxy.

Channel Four's controversial offer to Ferguson was a tribute not just to the latter's accomplishments as a historian. More significantly, it seemed designed to meet the pressing political requirement to rehabilitate the bearing of the "white man's burden" at the moment when the Anglo-American armies were poised to pick it up again with the lawless invasion of Iraq. The series and the choice of its presenter were set up to give the Empire's record a fresh lick of historical paint just when it was most needed. The same concern animates Roberts's book – flaky historical analogies are drawn between episodes in the Anglo-Saxon progress through the twentieth century and the Iraq War of the twenty-first at almost every opportunity, invariably to justify the Bush-Blair aggression.

The link between imperialisms past and present is made explicit at the end of Ferguson's *Empire*, the book based on his TV series and a work which presents an occasionally-nuanced but essentially high Victorian view of the adventure of the British Empire and its overall beneficent effects. Overall, Ferguson sets out to take the historiography of British imperialism back one hundred years or more, to the days of Macaulay and Seeley, when the Empire project was regarded, despite acknowledged excesses and problems, to have been beneficent because it spread British civilisation – or, and Ferguson is frank on this point, capitalism – across the world. [19]

Citing the work of Cooper and the speeches of Tony Blair, Ferguson argued that they "illustrate most clearly...how tenacious the grip of empire remains on the Oxford-educated mind." – his own not least. He then pointed out, accurately enough, that neither Blair's "international community" nor Cooper's European Union was able or willing to pick up the burden of Empire. "There is, however, only one power capable of playing an imperial role in the modern world, and that is the United States. Indeed, to some degree it is already playing that role." [20]

His only doubts concerned the resilience of the US in playing this appointed part: "...the American approach has too often been to fire some shells, march in, hold elections and then get the hell out – until the next crisis. Haiti is one recent example; Kosovo another. Afghanistan may yet prove to be the next."

This presentation was consistent with the two themes Ferguson struck from 9/11 onwards – the pressing need for a new imperialism and his doubts as to whether the US was up to the job. He was not far behind Paul Johnson in this respect, writing as early as October 2001: "The US has the resources, but does it have the guts to act as a global hegemon and make the world a more stable place? Imperialism is a dirty word, but when Tony Blair is essentially calling for the imposition of Western values – democracy and so on – it really is the language of liberal imperialism. Political globalisation is just a fancy word for...imposing your views and practices on others. The new imperialism is already in operation in Kosovo, Bosnia and East Timor." [21]

And just in case he had left any room for doubt, this in 2004: "I am fundamentally in favour of empire. Indeed, I believe that empire is more necessary in the 21st century than ever before." [22]

Roberts is if anything even more outspoken, and certainly less nuanced. "Imperialism is an idea whose time has come again" he exulted in the course of reviewing Deepak Lal's *In Praise of Empire*. Aping Ferguson, he argued that "the United States could bring untold benefits to the planet if only it could shrug off the notion...that empires are bad things per se." Roberts differs from pure neo-conservatism, however, in dismissing the idea that imperial rule should be a means of extending democracy (except when the expediency of endorsing the Bush rationale for invading Iraq requires otherwise). Democracy could lead to the wrong people taking charge. His imperialism is one of "economic globalisation and enforced order." [23]

On these grounds, he can assert that "The British empire was an exemplary force for good...the British gave up their empire largely without bloodshed, after having tried to educate their successor governments in the ways of democracy and representative institutions." Almost every assertion in this short passage is wrong, above all the view that Britain quit its colonies "largely without bloodshed", a view which involves ignoring India, Kenya, Malaya, Palestine, Aden, Cyprus, Iraq, Egypt and a good deal else besides. [24]

Roberts too makes plain his contemporary political intentions at the outset, which is to establish that "neo-conservatism is certainly no new historical departure in the self-proclaimed mission of the English-speaking peoples." To this end, the history of the twentieth century is reduced to a series of Manichean confrontations between the USA and the British Empire on the one hand and "Tirpitz's [German military leader in World War One] proto-fascism, Hitler's fascism, Soviet Red fascism, today's Islamo-fascism..." Fascism, fascism everywhere, except of course no "imperial-fascism" anywhere at all. [25]

Perhaps that is because Ferguson and Roberts both regard Empires as an immutable dimension of the human condition and therefore beyond the scope of moral criticism. "You might as well cast a moral judgement on rain as on the British Empire," Ferguson has written. Roberts' own outlook can be encapsulated in a passage dealing with Africa in his biography of Salisbury. The Tory imperialist is praised for his role in the notorious "scramble for Africa" thus: "Africa was carved up in a remarkably orderly manner, without provoking war between any of the European Powers involved. It was an admirable achievement...whatever the morality of this process − a modern concept which would not have detained Salisbury for very long...". Although Roberts shares the view that the history of Empire can be extracted from any framework for moral judgement, his own attitude that the violent colonisation of Africa was an achievement because no lives were lost in an undignified inter-European conflict does nevertheless betray a "moral" outlook of a sort. [26]

It may of course be convenient to remove the history of the British Empire from the scope of morality, given the nature of that record. But would Ferguson argue that, since "you might as well cast a moral judgement on rain as on the class struggle," the record of Communism is beyond judgement? It is only the belief systems of neo-conservative historians that are suspended above and beyond considerations of morality, apparently. Naturally, this view sustains the "neutralist" view of Empire, in which imperialism is regarded as intrinsically neither right nor wrong, but simply as a subject for sterile cost-benefit assessment.

Abstaining from moral judgement does not mean abstaining from political judgement, however. Here the key question is legitimacy. Ferguson admits excesses in the British campaign against the Mau-Mau in Kenya for example, but is clear that the colonisers were the lawful authority and that rising against them was, ipse facto, unacceptable. The key lies in his description of the Mau-Mau movement as a "violent insurrection" and later as a "civil war" waged by "rebels", without the slightest suggestion that it might have been legitimate for Kenyans to seek "land and freedom" from the colonialists. Likewise Roberts excuses the Amritsar massacre in India on the grounds that abstaining from murderous repression would have led to a still bloodier conflict as rebellion spread. In both cases, the imperialist had the right to act because the imperialist is the properly-constituted government, and that while the aspiration for national freedom may be acknowledged (most grudgingly in the case of Roberts) as quasi-legitimate, or maybe simply unavoidable, acting on that aspiration outside the parameters set by the colonial power (a power outside any form of democratic control), cannot be countenanced.

"Nobody, least of all me, claims that British imperial rule was perfect...but most sub-Saharan governments since independence have managed to treat their populations significantly worse than the British did," Ferguson wrote regarding Caroline Elkins's book critical of the British in Kenya. "Empires have their faults, no doubt. But independent African governments have often been more exploitative and worse for economic growth." The same line of reasoning (even were it an accurate representation to begin with) could be, and has been, used to justify almost every invasion and dictatorship. Economic growth in Nazi Germany, to take one example, was much stronger than it had been in the last years of Weimar. [27]

And a crude body-count calculus – or even the unsupported assertion of one – can substitute for an argued political case. Thus, a little light slaughter at Amritsar saved more lives by forestalling wider violence, Roberts argues. The same argument – that doing nothing would spare more lives – was used by Vichyites against the French resistance during World War Two, for example and could then, by extension, be further used to justify measures to crush that movement, Amritsar-style. But of course, Roberts sees some occupations by foreign powers as legitimate, and others as not. [28]

We shall look at the actual record of the British Empire shortly. But can this presentation be regarded as sound history? Many other contemporary historians have considerable criticisms of Ferguson and Roberts. For example, Kings College London historian Jon E Wilson described Ferguson as "the Leni Riefenstahl of George Bush's new imperial order. Just as Riefensthal's photography glorified the violence of fascism and sold it to the middle classes, Ferguson's Channel 4 series and book on the British empire presents the acceptable face of imperial brutality...Just as the world is preparing for a fresh Western war of conquest, Ferguson arrives to convince us that imperialism can be a Good Thing...Ferguson's arguments are misleading and dangerous...they encourage policy on a version of the history that is simply wrong." [29]

Cambridge University post-colonial studies expert Priyamvada Gopal sees "Ferguson's 'history' [as] a fairytale for our times which puts the white man and his burden back at the centre of heroic action. Colonialism – a tale of slavery, plunder, war corruption, land-grabbing, famines, exploitation, indentured labour, impoverishment, massacres, genocide and forced resettlement – is rewritten into a benign developmental mission marred by a few unfortunate accidents and excesses." [30]

The *Independent* columnist Johann Hari, a repentant supporter of the Iraq War, also confronted the race logic of Ferguson's pro-imperial views: "Whenever somebody argues that there are great swaths of humanity inherently incapable of self-rule who must be forever subject to imperial masters, it's an essential act of intellectual hygiene to condemn them...Ferguson does not tell us precisely who these people who must be always subject to colonial domination are. But I think we can assume that – like the servants and maids who waited on him as a child – they are black- and brown-skinned, bwana." *31*

Hari rather generously suggests that Ferguson's views might be merely a "quest for contrarianism" the term often applied to that song-and-dance man for the military-industrial complex, Christopher Hitchens. In fact, it shows far more consistency of political purpose. Perhaps he only wants to recreate the Kenyan colonial idyll of his youth, but his aim is not the stirring up of controversy about the Empire past as much as helping to impose an imperial future.

As for Roberts's cartoonish work on 20th century history, which so endeared him to the commanding heights of US conservatism, it was subjected to the most devastating review by Jacob Weisberg, the editor of US webzine Slate.com, in *The Financial Times*: "Mr Roberts views British colonialism and American hegemony as alike in their benevolence and effectiveness. Like Mr Bush, he is peevish that the recipients of such generosity are not more grateful.

"As a historian, Mr Roberts is present-minded in the extreme, returning at every stage to justifications for Mr Bush's actions in Iraq...Mr Roberts is already at work grafting Mr Bush's head on to Mr Churchill's body...Mr Roberts musters a muscular narrative, but examines nothing. All charges against the Anglo-American imperium are dismissed...as sloppy here as he is snobbish. I am seldom bothered by minor errors from a good writer, but Mr Roberts's mistakes are so extensive, fatuous and revealing of his basic ignorance about the US in particular...With this book Mr Roberts takes his place as the fawning court historian of the Bush administration...by producing a version of the past century that confirms its assumptions and prejudices." *32*

Lawrence James is less well-known than Ferguson or Roberts. He has however, authored works on the British Empire as a whole and on the Indian Raj which are unequivocal: "Britain's empire was a moral force and one for good. Few empires have equipped their subjects with the intellectual wherewithal to overthrow their rulers. None has been survived by so much affection and moral respect." So James does at least see the Empire as a "moral" question, in contradistinction to his colleagues, but one with a wholly positive answer. He fully shares in the historical fatuity that the end of the British Empire was "largely good-natured and involved little bloodshed," a position so at variance with the truth as to cast doubt on its author's entire professional judgement.[33]

Ferguson, Roberts and to a lesser extent James now dominate our airwaves and bookshops as the quasi-official dispensers of historical authority on the record of the British Empire. Television producers seems unconcerned at the almost total absence of any Asian, Arab or African historians who can be found to share their views.

Little wonder reasonable people are driven to distraction. As journalist Yasmin Alibhai-Brown wrote, after being excited to a high pitch of frustration through debating Ferguson and Roberts: "Those who claim Britain brought democratic values to their subjects need to name one colonised country where there was a credible democratic system during colonialism....

"This revisionism has been helped enormously by the empire-friendly media, the bland school curriculum...if you grew up white and in the colonies, especially Zimbabwe, you are considered exceptionally interesting by Radio 4 and others. The people who went through institutionalised mortification are invisible and inaudible. There isn't a single post-colonial historian today who has been given the media limelight."[34]

That is the whole point. History is a battle-field with no scope for vacillation or mixed messages. Once again "our boys" are planting the flag in foreign fields, taking the heathen firmly by the hand and leading him towards the sunlit tomorrow of free-market democratic capitalism. Even if some criticism of the "jolly old Empire" may be allowed among consenting academics, such dissent must not be permitted in front of the public and certainly never in view of the masses awaiting our liberating mission.

For that reason, it is now more important than ever to rescue the real record of the Empire from those who would like to bury it in obscurity and those who would like to use it as a model for contemporary world governance alike.

Chapter Two
Colonialists and Nazis

NAZI GERMANY on Trial – Good? Bad? The *BBC History Magazine* took the issue head on, examining each country conquered by Hitler's Germany and weighing up the record. In Poland, it was acknowledged, Nazi rule had been disastrous. However, the anschluss got the thumbs-up – most Austrians were happier under the Third Reich than they had been in their previous independent republic.

Of course, the *BBC History Magazine* did no such thing. The Nazis remain where they should be – beyond historical redemption. The good and bad of their regime is not a question on which the jury is still out. The BBC publication in fact put the British Empire on "trial" and asked if it was good or bad, touring the colonies in search of an answer. It found that British rule had – astonishingly – been "positive" in India, although admittedly negative in Jamaica, Iraq and Kenya. Egypt and South Africa were "too close to call". [1]

In Britain itself suggesting that the Empire deserves to be viewed in the same historical light as Nazi Germany seems far-fetched, or even offensive. Slavery might be accepted as a comparable evil at a push. But the "ordinary" workings of the Empire later on? Most British people would like to believe that 19th and 20th century colonialism operated on a more elevated moral plane all together. A similar opinion would probably be held amongst many people in the USA and Europe (who experienced the depredations of Hitler but not of colonialism), not to mention in Australia, Canada and New Zealand. Yet the comparison would not seem so far-fetched to the greater millions of subject people once ruled from London (or Paris, The Hague, Lisbon, Madrid, Brussels or Rome). That Hitler's regime is seen as the most bestial of modern times is not of course objectionable. What needs to be confronted, however, is the view that the crimes of other great powers of the last 150 years or so, being somehow less lurid and dramatic than those of the Nazis, can therefore be subject to a more nuanced judgement, in which the deaths of millions of people on the one hand can be offset against the construction of railways on the other.

This is not an entirely new argument, although it has seldom been made by white Europeans or Americans. The great African-American leader W.E.B. DuBois pointed out as long ago as 1947 that "there was no nazi atrocity – concentration camps, wholesale maiming and murder, defilement of women or ghastly blasphemy of childhood which Christian civilisation or Europe had not long been practising against colonial folk in all parts of the world in the name of and for the defence of a Superior race born to rule the world." [2]

The network of connections between imperialism in general, including the colonialism of Great Britain, on the one hand, and the crimes of the German regime between 1933 and 1945 on the other is an intimate one, ideologically and politically. But the bottom line is that the British Empire was almost certainly responsible for more human deaths, albeit over a considerably longer period of time, than Hitler was.

If we take the main charges levied by history against Hitler and Nazism – waging aggressive war, racism taken to the point of genocide, the suppression of democracy and the imposition of rule by force, the barbarous treatment of civilian populations, the establishment of concentration camps, medical experiments on prisoners, the disregard of treaties and law, ethnic cleansing, even hypocrisy and manipulation by means of deceitful propaganda – we can see that in each and every respect the former built on the example already set by British imperialism and the other colonial powers. Indeed, Nazism is essentially imperialism with the brakes taken off.

Of course, in many respects the Nazis took things further, and certainly the British Empire cannot match German fascist imperialism's record for massacre and aggression in a short twelve-year period. There is nothing in the British imperial record as chilling as the systematic extermination of the great majority of Europe's Jews in a period of little more than three years. And there was seldom a time when it was not at least possible for the victims of Empire, and those in Britain who supported them, to find a hearing in press and parliament. It should also be noted that if the British imperialists at least held out the eventual prospect of self-government or even independence to those people it ruled over, the Nazis envisaged eternal German domination of the conquered of Europe. However, on the broader scale, all imperialisms, and the most powerful British variant above all, have far more aspects in common with Nazism than those setting them apart.

Hitler is uniquely excoriated because his victims were almost all white Europeans, while those of Britain (and the other classic colonialisms – French, Belgian, Dutch, Italian and Wilhemine German itself) were Asian, African and Arab. As Aimé Césaire, the revolutionary from the French-controlled territory of Martinique, wrote of the "Christian bourgeois" in 1955: "What he cannot forgive Hitler for is not the crime in itself, the crime against man, it is not the humiliation of man as such, it is the crime against the white man, the humiliation of the white man, and the fact that he applied to Europe colonialist procedures which until then had been reserved exclusively for the Arabs of Algeria, the 'coolies' of India and the 'niggers' of Africa." More recently, a historian of Hitler's European empire, Mark Mazower, has also argued that the critical difference between the nazis and the European Empire-builders was that the former "simply set the fault line that divided rulers from ruled inside Europe and not outside it." [3]

In fact, the existing racist, authoritarian and militaristic impulses of the British Empire contained all the elements needed to fashion an indigenous Hitlerism had history of the early 20th century taken a different twist. Hitler himself was certainly not shy about expressing his admiration for the British Empire. When he wanted to teach the SS how they could rule an inferior race, he showed them the British film *Lives of a Bengal Lancer*. He lauded the British public-school system and what its scions had achieved in ruling India: "It is calculated to rear men of inflexible will and ruthless energy who regard intellectual problems as a waste of time but know human nature and how to dominate other men in the most unscrupulous fashion." When contemplating invading the USSR, he anticipated that "what India was for England, Russia will be for us." Even Niall Ferguson acknowledges Hitler's regard not only for the British Empire's accomplishments in exploiting natives but also for its consummate hypocrisy. [4]

And Hitler's great opponent Churchill was not the dictator's polar opposite as is generally presented – at least not in all his opinions. He was chided by one of his own ministers during the Second World War for having a "Hitler-like attitude" towards Indians. The British Premier held that Hindus were a "foul race" who were "protected by their mere pullulation from the doom that is their due". It is perhaps not surprising that many Indians during the war regarded the possibility of Hitler (or Japanese) rule as little worse than the reality of Churchill rule. [5]

Jomo Kenyatta, usually regarded as the father of Kenyan independence and by no means a militant or extreme opponent of the British, compared "the treatment of Africans by Britain's colonial fascists to that of the Jews by the Nazis," with, as we shall see, some justification. In fact, Kenya is one of the parts of the world where British rule was maintained by Hitlerite methods of uncontrolled racist violence even after the great war for freedom against fascism. [6]

Certainly, the leading British imperialists were the champions of almost every practice that Nazi ideology later raised to a fever pitch, and were inveterate enemies of democracy in their own country. It is no surprise to find, for example, that the pro-Nazi Lord Lothian, a leading figure in appeasement circles throughout the 1930s, had previously been a colonial administrator in South Africa. Such an overlap of views ran throughout the ruling class of the 1930s. Oxford University's older Fellows, Ferguson writes, "continued to think of Europe in the old imperialist terms of the 1890s, which was why they were inclined to accept Hitler's overtly racist arguments." The anti-semitism of the British establishment, if mild by the standards of a Streicher or a Goebbels, was nevertheless pervasive and Hitler's ill-treatment of Jews in the Reich before the war was never allowed to stand in the way of attempts to reach an Anglo-German understanding. [7]

So the analogy is not fanciful. Imperialism in general and its Nazi variant entwine at every point. The latter is the most extreme mutation of the former, so rehabilitating Curzon, Cromer and Milner is not different in kind from finding at least a few good points in the work of Rosenberg, Ribbentrop and Goering (as indeed many figures in the British establishment did at the time).

Taking the yardstick of Hitler Germany, the universally acknowledged ultimate measure of aggression and oppression, we can see how the British Empire, the great expression of British bourgeois civilisation, compares in relation to the four horsemen of the nazi-imperialist apocalypse: war; racism; state terror and the elimination (or suppression) of democracy and civil rights. On the way, we shall consider issues which emerge from any consideration of the Empire's actual record, like responsibility for the frequent famines. This unavoidably brief account draws particularly on the excellent recently-published works on the British Empire by historians Piers Brendon and John Newsinger.

Endless War

The British Empire's record was above all one of unending war. Colonial expansion was from the beginning accompanied by armed conflict – how could it be otherwise? There were 119 recorded wars for the sake of Empire in the 18th century and some seventy-two during Queen Victoria's reign in the nineteenth. The drive to create, expand further and then sustain the Empire made a most considerable contribution (through promoting imperial rivalry) to the outbreak of the two world wars of the 20th century, which also saw major colonial conflicts in South Africa, Kenya, Palestine, Malaya, Iraq, Egypt, Yemen and Ireland. Indeed, it is all but impossible to find a year in the imperial era during which Britain was entirely at peace. The requirement to establish and then protect imperial possessions across the world required endless war both against rivals anxious to share the spoils and, more persistently, the peoples of the subject territories themselves. [8]

The Royal Navy was the principal instrument of this policy at first. From the end of the nineteenth century and the Boer War unleashed by City commercial interests, the Army increasingly came to the fore. And the Air Force cut its teeth dropping bombs on Iraqi peasants a quarter century later. Their deployment was generally ordered without any consideration of whatever international law was prevailing at the time and they were promoted in their work by spurious justifications as self-serving as any used by later violators. China was attacked to allow its people to consume opium; Egypt was occupied to ensure it paid its debts; Nigeria (Yorubaland) was attacked to secure free entry of British goods and Ethiopia to permit free egress of British citizens. The Boer War was kicked off to protect the investments of London bankers and Afghanistan was invaded just in case anyone else got there first. A similar expediency has attended more recent wars from Korea (supposedly fought in support of the United Nations) to Iraq (fought in flat defiance of it). In many cases, wars were fought across the same territory more than once. The Ashanti may hold some sort of a record in being the other party in no less than eight British-initiated wars, all fought over what is now Ghana. The sixth was the crucial struggle, with British military victory being followed by the imposition of a massive indemnity to be rendered in gold. [9]

Whereas Hitler's aggression was confined to Europe, Europe was the only continent spared the worst of British imperialism by-and-large. The list of notable exceptions is even here a fairly long one, including as it does participation in the war to save Russia from socialism after the First World War, the intervention to save Greece from its own people after the Second and the occupations of Northern Ireland and Cyprus, plus the attack on Yugoslavia in our own times.

In sub-Saharan Africa aggressive war was waged in South Africa, Nigeria, Sierra Leone, Ghana and Kenya. In the Middle East – Egypt, Palestine, Yemen, Iraq and Iran. In the sub-continent, India itself and Afghanistan. In the Far East – China, Malaya, Burma, Korea and (little-remembered episodes) Vietnam and Indonesia in 1945-46, with British military involvement in Vietnam persisting for much longer. In the Western hemisphere, Guatemala/Belize, Guyana, and much of the Caribbean basin have been theatres of conflict. Going back a little further, Canada and the USA itself could be added to the roll. And this list omits smaller-scale "police actions" attendant on the need to keep order in the Empire.

In the light of this litany, it is clear the only novelty Hitler brought to war-making per se was his choice of battlefield and his extreme haste. On the point of principle, he was standing on the shoulders of Palmerston, Disraeli and Salisbury – and also, for sake of political balance, of Gladstone, Lloyd George and MacDonald. And as we shall see when we examine some of these conflicts in greater detail, the methods employed by the Empire to secure victory were generally more redolent of those deployed by the Nazis in the eastern theatre of Europe in the 1939-45 war than those it used in the Western.

Racism and Famine

The most important reason for this is the racist outlook common to British and German rulers throughout the imperial period. As we have seen, Churchill did not view a Hindu so very differently from how Hitler saw a Pole, or even a Jew, even if his racism did not and could not lead to such genocidal conclusions. His outlook was not unusual – such attitudes ran through the whole enterprise of imperialism, which placed life-and-death power over millions of people in the hands of individuals of considerably less scruple and intelligence than Churchill and, furthermore, insulated them from even that measure of parliamentary scrutiny and accountability to which MPs in Britain itself were subject. In the words of the famous medical journal *The Lancet* in 1865, the natives had either "to be constantly kept down with a rod of iron or slowly exterminated." [10]

Exercising such power without control over other peoples both requires and reinforces racism. Bayly and Harper, in their work on Britain's post-war Asian empire, tell the story of Derek van den Boegarde, a captain in the British Army who, having taken part in the liberation of the Bergen-Belsen concentration camp, was redeployed east for what was intended, pre-Hiroshima, to be the final great offensive against Japan. Disembarking at Calcutta station he saw an Indian porter being beaten by a "fat, ginger-haired, moustached, red-faced, stocky little major from Transport. Screaming. Thrashing at the cringing Indian with his swagger cane....My first sight and sound of the Raj at work." Fifty years later the officer found the memory more repulsive than the desolation of Germany. It requires no great leap of the imagination to see in that officer – again, no atypical figure in colonial life – the outline of the concentration camp guard. [11]

This exercise of raw, brutal, racial power was the political cornerstone of Empire. A colonial governor in Australia reported to Gladstone that Queenslanders "of culture and refinement, of the greatest humanity and kindness to their fellow whites...talk not only of the *wholesale* butchery...but of the *individual* murder of natives, exactly as they would talk of a day's sport...," as the Aboriginal people were put to the sword. [12]

So it went, across continents and generations. "No Dogs, No Chinese" read the sign at the entrance to a Shanghai park. A former black-and-tan soldier serving as a policeman in Palestine in the 1930s observed that "running over an Arab is the same as a dog in England except we do not record it." In India towards the end of the war against fascism one British officer boasted of having had "jolly good fun" having "shot down 24 niggers himself" while fighting nationalist demonstrators. [13]

This racism was unabashed. Thus Sir Godfrey Huggins, the Prime Minister of Southern Rhodesia (now Zimbabwe) in the 1930s: "It is time for people in England to realise that the white man in Africa is not prepared and never will be prepared to accept the African as an equal, socially or politically." Such examples from colonial leaders could be cited *ad nauseam*.) [14]

Racism was central to every aspect of imperial rule, with all native peoples, other than those tiny elites which were nurtured in order to better secure imperial rule, reduced to helot status. Their well-being (indeed, their lives) were entirely subordinate to the economics and politics of the imperialist system. And racism was, of course, used as an instrument of division among the colonised, with different ethnic groups seen as being locked in eternal conflicts which could only be contained by beneficent British rule. If such a conflict ever seemed to be abating, imperial rule usually found a way to stoke it up again. It is also reflected in the view of the colonised as "primitive" or "children," ignoring when not actually destroying their indigenous cultural inheritance. [15]

What other than racism could underpin the ethnic cleansing carried out in our own time by a British Labour government, when it deported the entire native population of Diego Garcia to facilitate their homeland's conversion into a US military base? It is, on balance, safe to assume that the population of, say, Dorking would not have been so inconvenienced. Considerations of the system's smooth functioning overrode at more or less every turn the humanitarian, Christian or philanthropic principles which some colonial officials undoubtedly held. This is clearest in relation to the issue of famine which blighted many parts of the Empire – India and Ireland above all.

The famine in Ireland of 1845-47 exemplified the emerging synthesis of racism and capitalist economics. It is commonly held that the mass starvation which reduced the population of Ireland by almost a half was a result of the failure of the potato crop. This is only half the story. Such a crop failure was general across Europe – but only in colonial Ireland did it lead to famine. As communist historian T.A. Jackson asserts "the amount of corn, cattle etc exported from Ireland in these years would have fed all those who hungered twice over." That the people were not in fact fed was due to the absolute priority given by the government in London to maintaining the social position of the landlord class in Ireland. This in turn was only possible if the Irish peasant was regarded as all but subhuman, condemned by class and then super-condemned by race and religion to occupy an inferior place in the imperial scheme of things. [16]

"Britain relied on the panaceas of Adam Smith – private enterprise and market forces. So while peasants starved, ships full of Irish corn sailed for England, which sent troops rather than food to quell protestors," Brendon records. Very limited charitable relief was eventually mobilised, but even this was too much for *The Times*, which feared that such benevolence would impede Ireland's moral progress! Christian philanthropy was, not for the last time in the history of the Empire, confounded by bourgeois misanthropy. [17]

This atrocity was reproduced on a still larger scale in the course of British rule in India – the star in the Empire, and for more than a century the pivot on which Britain's world role turned. The British Empire had more colonial subjects in the Indian Raj (which also included the territory of contemporary Pakistan, Bangladesh and Burma) than everywhere else put together. It would have had still more but for the mass starvations colonialism presided over once every generation or so – but have never recurred since the sub-continent secured its independence.

As Mike Davis outlines in his outstanding book *Late Victorian Holocausts* anything from twelve to 29 million people died from starvation across India in the famines largely caused by the structures of economic development imposed by the Raj and greatly exacerbated by *laissez-faire* dogma and official indifference, which as in Ireland, often extended to the point of actual obstruction of any relief effort which might distort "normal" – i.e. market – economics.

The extension of capitalism into India during the nineteenth century worsened the pre-existing problem of famine in Indian life. "In the first half of the nineteenth century there were seven famines, with an estimated total of

1.5 million deaths from famine. In the second half of the nineteenth century there were twenty-four famines…with an estimated total, according to official records, of over 20 million deaths," the leading Marxist authority on India R. Palme Dutt wrote. Humanity was sacrificed to economy and, in the words of Viceroy Lord Curzon, "excited no more attention in Britain than a squall on the Serpentine." [18]

Those famous railroads, so often hailed as the great bequest of British civilisation to the sub-continent, also played a nefarious role, quite at odds with the mythology. As well as earning British capital a fabulous rate of return they were used to shift desperately-needed food away from the famine-afflicted regions, and then expedite the arrival of troops travelling in the other direction to suppress starvation-related disorder. As Keir Hardie told the House of Commons, "railways had increased the cost of living and the land tax; they made possible the carrying-off of the surplus grain grown in plentiful years so that in seasons of scarcity there were no reserves to fall back on as in pre-railway days." [19]

Indeed, peasant rebels sometimes targeted railways for destruction, viewing them as key links in the system of colonial oppression. It was the imposition of the "free market" (with built-in distortions to privilege the interests of British capital) on traditional economies which bears the responsibility for creating the catastrophe, and the prevailing British power for superintending it. That free-market system was itself ultimately oriented towards the extraction of super-profit for British interests – by the end of the nineteenth century, India was remitting £10 million a year to Britain in interest payments (£6 million from those famous railways alone) while a further £10 million was being paid in salaries and pensions to the British rulers of the Raj. Any development was secondary and incidental to that overarching aim of removing as much wealth as possible as fast as possible, something British free-booters from Clive onwards had proved singularly adept at. The extension of the same system under British coercion produced similar results in Egypt and elsewhere. If the flag followed capital, starvation followed the flag in turn. [20]

Nor was famine in India merely a relic of the Victorian era. It persisted as an element of life right down to (but not beyond) the end of the Raj. The famine in Bengal in 1943 saw 3.5 million people die from starvation. Described by contemporary Indian nationalists as the "fulfilment of British rule in India," it was the worst single episode of starvation there since the 1770s. Dutt wrote: "The famine was a 'man-made' famine. The shortage in Bengal was only a shortage of six weeks supplies and could have been made up by imports and equitable distribution. But...the entire stocks had been cornered by big zamindars and traders, and the corrupt bureaucracy rather than force stocks out of their hands helped them to shoot up prices and play havoc with the lives of millions of people." [21]

The Viceroy, Lord Linlithgow, was accused of a "callous disregard of duty" by a former member of his governing Council. As Maria Misra records "the war cabinet in London was warned in early 1942 of the impending crisis, but refused to stop the export of food from Bengal or to divert shipping to bring supplies to India." The three million or more people dying (far in excess of total British war deaths by way of a comparison) were dismissed at the time by Churchill's unashamedly racist scientific adviser Lord Cherwell as a "statistical invention," Churchill himself regarded famine relief as appeasement of the Indian National Congress and in any case "the starvation of anyway underfed Bengalis is less serious [than that of] sturdy Greeks," thereby underlining his contempt for those Indian people who he was obsessed with keeping under British rule. Again, this is not a world view radically different from the fascist brutality displayed towards the Slav peoples of eastern Europe and the USSR during the second world war. [22]

Of course, it is still argued, not least by Ferguson *et al*, that it is not legitimate to lay the blame for these millions of death on the British government. Ferguson, for example, attributes the several million deaths in the Bengal famine of 1943 to the usual "combination of incompetence, complacency and indifference, tinged with resentment at the previous year's riots" leading to an "inadequate" official response. This is a mealy-mouthed apology for an immense human calamity. [23]

In fact, since the three Prime Ministers who presided over the worst famines in India were Disraeli, Salisbury and Churchill, holding London responsible would require treating the three great icons of pre-Thatcher Conservatism as mass murderers. While desperate to avoid anything tending towards such a conclusion, neo-conservative historians take the exact opposite view when it comes to famines in socialist countries. There, the weather, the stage of social development and human error are not allowed to enter into the calculation at all. Only government should be held to account. The deaths attributed to the Soviet famines of the early 1930s or the Chinese of the late 1950s are thus invariably added to the death tolls laid at the door of Stalin or Mao. But those in India are not hung around the necks of the Tory leadership.

As Peter Wilby pointed out in the *New Statesman*: "...if we are to hold Stalin and Mao responsible for the millions who starved as a result of their socialist agricultural policies...we ought to hold the British empire's rulers responsible for those who starved as a result of *laissez-faire* policies. Equally, if we are to defend the British, as [Lawrence] James does, by pointing out that our colonial subjects held us in such esteem that they adopted our laws and even came to live here, we should also note that millions of former Soviet citizens revere Stalin to this day." [24]

The difference does not actually lie in the area of responsibility at all. It lies in the view of the imperial court historians that the Empire was legitimate and that free-market economics are the natural order of things, while socialism is an aberrant departure from the laws of human development. Here a class outlook concerning the relative value of systems of society buttresses the racial view of the relative value of lives of different people.

This view of the world was anticipated by Karl Marx in 1847. As he put it in *The Poverty of Philosophy*: "Economists have a singular method of procedure. There are only two kinds of institutions for them, artificial and natural. The institutions of feudalism are artificial institutions, those of the bourgeoisie are natural institutions...every religion which is not theirs is an invention of men, while their own is an emanation from God. When the economists say that present-day relations – the relations of bourgeois production – are natural, they imply that these are the relations in which wealth is created and productive forces developed in conformity with the laws of nature. These relations are themselves natural laws independent of the influence of time. They are eternal laws which must always govern society." Only substitute historians for economists, and one has the outlook of Ferguson, Roberts and James in all its myopia. [25]

Undeveloping the World

We should now address further the pro-imperial argument that Empire, however rapacious or brutal it may sometimes have been, was nevertheless good for economic development. Andrew Roberts insists that "the British empire delivered astonishing growth rates, at least in those places fortunate enough to be coloured pink on the globe." [26]

The truth is different – in fact, imperialism contributed little or nothing to development in the countries it subjected. Naturally, this is a minefield of disputed statistics and, as Nicholas Dirks writes in relation to the consequences of the Raj, "the argument over how to interpret the economic data concerning the impact of the British presence on India hinges on whether one views the colonial state as legitimate and benevolent, or as fundamentally extractive in a way no indigenous state could be." [27]

But the evidence that imperialism, far from promoting economic advance, actually undeveloped the colonies is overwhelming. According to one student of the Raj "under British rule the life expectancy or ordinary Indians fell by 20%, while India's per capita income did not rise from 1757 to 1947." Mike Davis also finds there was no increase in per capita income at all in India in those years, while even Ferguson admits that "…the average Indian had not got much richer under British rule. Between 1757 and 1947 British per capita gross domestic product increased in real terms by 347 per cent, Indian by a mere 14 per cent. A substantial share of the profits which accrued as the Indian economy industrialised went to British managing agencies, banks or shareholders; this despite the fact that there was no shortage of capable Indian investors and entrepreneurs." [28]

It was under British rule that the Bengal economy, highly-developed by prevailing world standards, went into unremitting decline and sank into the poverty from which it has yet to emerge to this day. Dirks estimates that by the end of the eighteenth century the colonialism superintended by the East India Company was removing around nine per cent of Bengal's GDP annually through distorted trade, taxation and plain robbery. These millions extorted and exported not only crippled the local economy, they also provided the foundations for fabulous fortunes which came to play a vast and corrupting role in British politics itself. [29]

This is the invariable consequence of the enforced introduction of capitalism. Mike Davis points out that India and China's textile industries were overcome "not so much by market competition as they were forcibly dismantled by war, invasion, opium and a Lancashire-imposed system of one-way tariffs". The existing indigenous institutions collapsed before this onslaught, which was above all designed to separate the labourer from the land and thereby turn both into commodities. As Maria Misra puts it "just as the British had enclosed their own common lands in the seventeenth century...so also in India they determinedly privatised what had been public and made exclusive what had been common." [30]

Harvard economist Jeffrey Frieden puts his estimate for the British contribution to India's development in between Davis's zero and Ferguson's 14 per cent: "The most careful estimates available indicate that in 1950 Indian output per person was less than 10 per cent higher than it had been a century earlier." That per capita output in India then grew by fifty per cent in the next 25 years alone despite a very rapid increase in population is a sweeping refutation of Roberts's paean of praise to the Empire's "astonishing" economics. And when there was both economic growth and a retention of significant revenues in a particular colony – such as in Burma in the years before the war – this was largely used to secure "bigger salaries and perks for British expatriates," in Bayly and Harper's analysis. The special contribution of Britain to China's development was the forcible opening up of its territory to the opium trade, the better to balance India's accounts with the City, and the imposition of a broad range of privileges for itself and other imperial powers. The legal import of opium persisted until 1917, and the exploitative commercial privileges until 1942, despite the growing national struggle of the Chinese people. [31]

And what was true of India, China and Burma was truer still of Africa. Statistics furnished to the House of Commons in 1927 revealed that the consuming power of the natives of the Ciskei had fallen by half over the preceding fifty years, even as the gold and diamond mines of the territory expanded production by leaps and bounds. Copper exported from what is now Zambia in 1937, for example, generated £5.5 million in dividends and royalties for British shareholders out of total revenue of £12 million. The share paid to African labour was just £244,000. Tobacco exports from Malawi (Nyasaland) at the same time yielded around £1,000 for every European employed as against £1.65 for each African. Ghana exported minerals to the value of £5,558,000 in 1937, of which £3,000,000 went in profits. Taxes bore most heavily on the native population throughout Africa. It was in the hope, largely fulfilled until overtaken by military defeat, of reproducing these rapacious rates of return that German big business so enthusiastically backed Hitler's conquest of eastern Europe during World War Two. [32]

Guyanese anti-colonial writer Walter Rodney has outlined in detail how the African colonies were pillaged to prop up the imperial balance of payments. By 1955, Africa's contribution to Britain's foreign exchange position amounted to just a little less than three-quarters of the total – this was a wealth transfer from some of the poorest parts of the planet. "...What was called the 'development of Africa' by the colonialists was a cynical shorthand expression for the 'intensification of colonial exploitation of Africa to develop capitalist Europe.'" In every colony, as a matter of policy, indigenous routes to industrialisation were blocked off, monocultural crop economies were imposed on the widest scale possible, forced labour utilised to maximise profit to capitalist investors and the entire course of development subordinated to the needs of the imperial power. And, once more, the railroad system was designed with only Empire in mind – routes were planned with a view to extracting wealth from the interior, not to developing intra-African economic intercourse. Interest payments on railway investment swallowed up one-third of the revenue of colonial Africa in the 1930s. The railways offered preferential rates for the carriage of European-controlled exports, while charging higher fares for the transit of African agricultural implements. [33]

Moreover, the development of the then-superfluous Uganda railway required in turn the development of white settlement in Kenya if trade was to be generated to make the line viable, thereby laying the foundation for one of the worst episodes in Britain's late-colonial occupation of Africa, described below. [34]

Nigeria, particularly its northern regions, was Britain's most populous African colony and one with perhaps the greatest potential for endogenous economic development. Yet at independence in 1960, manufacturing and processing accounted for less than four per cent of GDP, while 70 per cent of the country's savings and all of its industry were in the control of foreign banks. Such social development as had been introduced was primarily oriented towards perpetuating this system of dependence with, it must be said, some success.[35]

Two further aspects of colonialism in Africa invite comparison with nazism. First, there was the explicit aim of establishing a form of lebensraum – living space – for white people on the land. Just as Hitler saw sturdy German farmers cultivating the land of Poland and the Ukraine, with the natives merely supplying necessary menial labour, so did British colonialism envisage white settlement across Africa. "Alienation of African land is the first principle of European colonisation. Unless this were so, whites could not settle in the tropics with any great prospect of solid profits from large-scale farming," wrote anti-imperialist author George Padmore in 1948. Such settler communities were later to be the source of most of the violent resistance to decolonisation – or even the suggestion of African advancement. Happy were those colonies in West Africa blessed with the Anopheles and Aedes-Aegypti mosquitoes, carriers of malaria and yellow fever respectively. Their attentions made their lands unsuitable for large-scale white colonisation, sparing the indigenous population the terrors of settler rule.[36]

Second, there was the super-exploitation of native labour, including of children. The Juveniles Employment Act passed in Rhodesia was typical. It was justified by the government as being "in the best interests of the children, as it prevents them becoming vagabonds and waifs exposed to pernicious influences." Vagabondage was, of course, the inevitable consequence of the seizure of land and the coercion of the native population into wage labourers. The Act was enforced with flogging, and over 1,000 children were so punished in 1938 alone.

Nor was colonial education a pathway to development. In British-ruled Africa, on average roughly sixty times as much was spent on the schooling of each European child as was allotted to each African child, although figures vary somewhat from one country to another. If this was not quite a Goering-standard view of education – "education is dangerous, every educated person is a future enemy" – it was along that line. All the settler community required was mute and compliant manual labourers. [37]

So if Africa is today a "scar on the conscience of humanity", as Tony Blair liked to say, then it reflects in overwhelming measure the wounds inflicted in the time of colonialism. Any programme of alleviating it through a return of neo-colonial governance will produce no better results.

State Violence

The intense exploitation of the peoples of Africa and Asia could only be sustained by violence against the native peoples in general, and most especially any that appeared to be in danger of getting out of hand. US imperial pundit Thomas Friedman's oft-quoted aphorism "the hidden hand of the market will never work without that hidden fist" that is the US military would not have come as news to Victorian Empire-builders. Their enterprise was founded on mass killing and this was not an element which diminished as time went on.[38]

Again, the great uprising in India of 1857 appears as a turning point, when the illusion that British rule could depend on notions of superior civilisation was replaced by the reality that it depended on superior artillery and brutality. One officer alone, Colonel James Neil, executed six thousand people at Allahabad in the course of suppressing the Indian national movement; more than the entire British losses sustained in what Victorian opinion was pleased to style a "mutiny" (although the only lawful authority in India, the Mughal of Delhi, was in fact a supporter of the uprising against the depredations of the East India Company's governance). [39]

This same Neill, who was of the opinion that "the Word of God gives no authority to the modern tenderness for human life", further put his Christian understanding into practice by burning sepoys alive, or by way of variation forcing them to eat beef and pork before sewing them into pigskins and hanging them. For good measure, Hindus were then buried and Muslims burned, the better to outrage the traditions of both religions. [40]

Racism again underpinned the actions of those homicidal officers, much as it did in the German Army nearly a century later. The "peculiar aggravation of the Cawnpore massacres," editorialised *The Times* in reference to the killing of white civilians during the uprising, was "that the deed was done by a subject race – by black men who dared to shed the blood of their masters." The sentiment of the entire British press was savage, like "an American Slave-state newspaper" according to Governor-General Lord Canning. This attitude was put into practice on the ground. A soldier writing in the *Bombay Telegraph* at the time made it clear that there was no such thing as a "good Indian": "All the city people found within the walls [of Delhi] when our troops entered were bayoneted on the spot...They were not mutineers, but residents of the city, who trusted to our well-known mild rule for pardon. I am glad to say they were to be disappointed." [41]

No less an imperial notable than Lord Palmerston demanded that Delhi be erased from the earth altogether after the uprising had been put down. "...every civil building connected with the Mohammedan tradition should be levelled to the ground without regard to antiquarian veneration or artistic predilections," he said in words which prefigure Hitler's stated intentions towards Leningrad in 1941. The Nazi leader was thwarted in his ambitions by the Soviet army. Palmerston's plan was largely put into effect, its complete realisation being halted only by practical rather than ethical considerations. Possibly as many as 100,000 "mutineers" were massacred in all. [42]

This behaviour established the template to be used over the next 150 years by the British for handling native insurrection against imperial rule. Those resisting are presented by the metropolitan media and political classes in starkly racist terms, stripping them not only of the justice inherent in their cause but even of their humanity. Then the way is cleared, ideologically speaking, for violent repression unbounded by any normal "rules of war" or considerations of moral scruple. This has been the essential pattern from India to China to Kenya to Malaya to Iraq, from that day to this. This does not, of course, exclude a role for window-dressing and various forms of political hoopla. After 1857 a cult of British royalty was sedulously nurtured among the "rajah class" in India – essential intermediaries in imperial rule – to bind them more closely to their real overlords. Andrew Roberts's idol Lord Salisbury said such publicity would hide "the nakedness of the sword upon which we really rely." Salisbury was more severely realistic than his apologists in the 21st century are for their own wars. [43]

And the sword it was from then forward, right down to the very end of the Raj – most famously at Amritsar, where the murderous suppression of an unarmed demonstration was followed by a regime of collective punishment and organised humiliation by the British authorities, including cutting off water and electricity supplies and forcing Indians to crawl along the main street on their stomachs. There was also the now-routine aerial bombardment of surrounding villages. [44]

In the early 1930s, over 100,000 Indian freedom fighters were held in British prisons. Massacres were commonplace – 65 killed in Peshawar on April 23 1930, with 150 wounded; 25 killed and 100 wounded in Sholapur on May 8 of the same year; 141 killed and 386 wounded in Cawnpore on March 24 1931; 47 killed and 134 wounded in Karachi on March 19 1935. Any one of these slaughters would be recalled forever had white Europeans been the victims. Tens of thousands more Indians were killed and wounded protesting or resisting British rule during World War Two, a conflict "for democracy" which most Indian nationalist leaders sat out in jail. 60,000 political activists were imprisoned in 1946, and 14,000 were still there two years later. There were, Brendon writes, "occasional atrocities reminiscent of 1857," and medical experiments were carried out on detainees held in the Andhara Islands. It is scarcely surprising that post-war attempts by the British to take punitive measures against Indians who had served in the Indian National Army, which fought alongside the Japanese in the hope of thereby securing independence, were unpopular across Indian society. [45]

Although there were not national movements on the Indian example in most of Africa before the 1939 war, there was no shortage of state violence. Who in Europe now remembers the name of the Reverend John Chilembwe? Along with twenty others he was executed in Nyasaland (now Malawi) in 1915 for leading a revolt against exploitation and repression on the big estates. Or the 32 women killed at Opobo and the 18 at Utu-Etim-Expo, both in Nigeria in 1929, for protesting against colonial taxation policy, which in Nigeria as elsewhere bore heavily on the natives while leaving the colonial companies more or less untouched? As the official inquiry into the latter incidents noted, "we must understand that the women persuaded themselves that they were not only the victims of outrageous oppression but faced with absolute ruin." Life itself, it might be said, had actually persuaded the brave Nigerian women of this. [46]

Writing shortly before the outbreak of World War Two, British anti-imperialist author Leonard Barnes summed up the contemporary position: "There has been bloodshed, sometimes quite extensive, in Northern Rhodesia, South Africa, Zanzibar, Mauritius, Tanagnyika, St. Lucia, Trinidad, Barbados, Jamaica. In India and Burma repression by shooting is endemic. There has been the great strike and boycott movement in the Gold Coast; in Cyprus large-scale arrests of working-class leaders and dismissal of officials with liberationist views... in August 1938 the Rangoon riots resulted in 150 killed and over 500 injured. In Palestine the British have been for years at open war with the inhabitants." [47]

One of the cornerstone Ferguson-James-Roberts myths (drawing on pre-existing dogma among orthodox imperial historians) is that of "peaceful decolonisation" of the Empire which ended without a bloodbath. The Nazis, of course, had to be compelled by violence to disgorge every territory they had conquered. They left nowhere voluntarily. As we have seen, the imperial historians allege that the British attitude was different and that colonies passed peacefully into independence without obstruction from the "mother country."

Not so. In one case after another (Ireland being the most celebrated) the demand for national independence from Britain was met with fearful violence, begetting in turn the violence of those who were denied any democratic means of expression. This violence persisted right down to the moment of British departure in many cases. "During the Macmillan government there were riots, strikes or boycotts, often violent, in Sierra Leone, Uganda, Nyasaland [Malawi], Zanzibar, British Guiana and Brunei," Ronald Hyam records. [48]

Kenya is an unambiguous example of the British determination to resist decolonisation or, when it became unavoidable, to control it through extreme coercion. Caroline Elkins's scrupulous analysis of the British campaign against the Mau-Mau, the liberation movement based among the Kikuyu peoples of Kenya deprived of both "land and freedom" to cite their slogan, concludes that there was in 1950s Kenya "a murderous campaign to eliminate Kikuyu people, a campaign that left tens of thousands, perhaps hundreds of thousands, dead." [49]

One Asian lawyer who represented detainees, Fitz de Souza, goes even further: "I would say there were several hundred thousand killed…One hundred easily, though more likely two to three hundred thousand." Ms Elkins's own demographic analysis finds "somewhere between 130,000 and 300,000 Kikuyu are unaccounted for." Certainly, the official figure of "only" 11,000 Mau Mau killed is totally implausible. There is a difficulty in establishing the definitive figure in that British government records from the Colonial Office have been systematically "cleansed" the better to conceal the truth. [50]

The basic outlines of the story are nevertheless well-known. British settlers seized 12,000 square miles of Kenyan land in the first half of the 20th century, much of it distributed by the British authorities to sundry peers of the realm in a brazenly corrupt process, while confining 1.25 million Kikuyus to 2,000 square miles. This circumstance was exacerbated by the complete lack of any form of representative democracy in the colony and the repression of peaceful African attempts to seek redress. Indeed, Kenyan Africans were twice quite explicitly betrayed by the London government – a solemn promise by Ramsey MacDonald not to permit encroaching on established Native Reserves was discarded when one of the latter was found to contain gold reserves, and a pledge by Churchill's wartime government to ensure "equal representation" of Africans on the colony's governing councils (itself obviously a formula for white over-representation) was abandoned by the 1945 Labour government under settler pressure. It is scarcely surprising that this record of misrule and deception eventually provoked rebellion as Kenyan soldiers returned home after fighting for European freedom in World War Two to find themselves third-class citizens in their own land. [51]

Massacre and the internment of around 320,000 Kikuyu in concentration camps were used to put down the Mau-Mau insurrection, with the lavish use of torture and the rule of law effectively discarded. Jomo Kenyatta, the more moderate nationalist leader was imprisoned after a farcical trial in which the British judge, Ransley Thacker, was bribed by the Governor with £20,000 (ten times his annual salary) to deliver a guilty verdict. [52]

Another scrupulous author, David Anderson, examined 900 records of capital cases brought against alleged Mau-Mau by the colonial authorities and concluded "that there was widespread beating and torture of suspects, that defendants rarely had a chance to prepare a defence, and that judges were racially biased in their evaluation of evidence." The exercise of British jurisprudence included mass trials, with defendants numbered instead of named. Confessions extracted under duress were used in 80 per cent of cases, all of which were followed by mass executions. [53]

Police reserve forces drawn from among the white settlers "took the emergency as a licence to kill. They hunted down 'Kikuyu trouble-makers' like wild animals. They tortured them at will, sometimes castrating men and raping women. They exterminated them without mercy." British soldiers were paid five shillings (equal to $9 in today's money) for each Kikuyu male they killed. As proof, they sometimes nailed the limbs of African guerrillas to crossroads posts. The police not only carried out targeted assassinations but also massacred civilians in cold blood, the innocent alongside the "guilty." Some settlers openly advocated genocide, either by dropping the atom bomb on Kikuyus, or poisoning their drinking wells. The British state's leaders may have deprecated the extremism of Ferguson's settler community, but they systematically and violently intervened to protect the settlers' social position and property rights.[54]

The Special Branch became known as the "Kenyan SS" and one settler in the Rift Valley was dubbed the "Doctor Mengele of Kenya" for measures including "burning the skin of live Mau Mau suspects and forcing them to eat their own testicles." On arrival at concentration camps detainees were greeted with the same initiation ceremony as greeted new arrivals at Dachau – running a "gauntlet of baton-wielding guards." One Assistant Police Commissioner, Duncan McPherson said conditions "were worse than anything I experienced in my four and a half years as a prisoner of the Japanese." The murder and sexual abuse of prisoners was commonplace. Parliament in Britain was systematically deceived as to what was going on – although relatively few MPs were interested to begin with. Efforts to secure compensation for survivors of this regime have proceeded unavailingly since. [55]

All of this nazi-type behaviour took place in the 1950s, after the great war against fascism and the exposure of Hitler's atrocities. As much as anything else it shows how stubborn and deep-rooted are the barbarities associated with imperial rule.

In Malaya in the same period, British rule faced a Communist-led national liberation movement. There, as throughout the Far East, British rule (and prestige) had collapsed before the Japanese in 1942, to the overwhelming indifference of the ruled. Communism was attractive to the mass of Malayan peoples, at least in part because its message of class solidarity provided a means of overcoming the ethnic and racial differences sedulously nurtured by the British. Imperial power was reimposed on the country, post-Hiroshima, largely in order to secure control over the country's considerable supplies of rubber, a strategic and profitable commodity (the most important dollar earner for the beleaguered Empire at the time), and also to prevent undesirable developments like the nationalisation of the British-owned Burmah Oil Company. It is notable that the 1945 Labour government, great nationalisers at home, were reluctant to extend the same right to the peoples of the colonies – an unpleasant trait which resurfaced when, in opposition, it condemned Egypt's takeover of the Suez Canal. [56]

To these ends a violent campaign was directed against the Communists, who had earlier earned British commendation for their part in the anti-Japanese struggle. Indeed, Chin Peng, the leader of the Communist Party of Malaya, took part in the Empire's victory parade before the King in London! These services rendered counted for nothing when the Malayan liberation movement took the view that freedom meant freedom from the British as well as the Japanese. Many of the techniques of counter-insurgency warfare were first tried out against the unfortunate Malayans, including forced resettlement. There was "no human activity from the cradle to the grave that the police did not superintend." The British commanding officer General Templer imposed a regime on the country which was described by contemporary Cambridge historian Victor Purcell, an expert on Malaya, as "quasi-fascist." [57]

Villages were burnt and collective punishment handed out prodigiously. Army units engaged in a grim competition to see who could kill most insurgents. One British officer said: "We were shooting people...killing them...This was raw savage success. It was butchery. It was horror." While Malaya eventually won its formal independence, the domination of British business interests was maintained into the post-colonial period by these methods, forever symbolised by photographs printed in the *Daily Worker* of grinning British soldiers holding aloft the heads of slaughtered partisans. All together over 10,000 people were killed, 34,000 interned and 15,000 deported. A senior police official admitted that conditions were "worse than that experienced by internees under the Jap regime", long the benchmark in Britain for brutality towards prisoners. The emergency also had its own My Lai – 26 rubber industry workers murdered in cold blood by the Scots Guards at Batang Kali in 1948. [58]

226 members of the Communist Party were hanged for fighting for their national and social emancipation. Among those executed – for possession of a weapon – was the President of the Federation of Trade Unions S.A. Ganapathy. As was the case in Kenya, most government files relating to the "emergency" were subsequently destroyed, including, of course, those relating to Batang Kali. [59]

Malaya was by such means secured as a counterweight to the radically-oriented Indonesia of the time, a strategic consideration which was eventually rendered otiose by the massacre of one million Indonesian Communists at the instigation of the CIA and the installation of the right-wing Suharto dictatorship in 1965.

Cyprus, too, had to secure its independence in the teeth of British-instigated bloodbaths every step of the way. Set against the Empire's strategic interests, the views of the peoples of the island counted for nothing, the more so since so many of them (across Greek and Turkish communities) had started supporting the communist party AKEL. Anthony Eden put it crudely in the 1950s: "No Cyprus, no certain [military] facilities to protect our supply of oil. No oil, hunger and unemployment in Britain. It is a simple as that." It is probably not too cynical to see oil company profits as weighing as much in Eden's considerations as "hunger and unemployment". [60]

Eden's candour was matched by that of the chief of the Imperial General Staff, Sir John Harding, who was dispatched to rule Cyprus in 1955. If the Cypriots were not to be allowed to democratically govern themselves – and that decision had been taken – then "a regime of military government must be established and the country run indefinitely as a police state." And so it was.

Divisions between the two communities were, of course, exacerbated and exploited, and auxiliary forces recruited to institute a reign of terror against socialists, communists, progressives and nationalists alike. The historian Robert Holland is cited by Perry Anderson in an exhaustive article on the issue as observing that "...it was the British who, in the first instance, had to screw the Turks up to a pitch of excitement about Cyprus, not the other way around." Eventually Cyprus was allowed what Anderson accurately describes as a "neutered independence" hedged in with so many caveats and safeguards for British and NATO interests as to reduce its government to the level of autonomy of a County Council. But the scene had been set for the Turkish invasion of 1974 which instituted a partition, accompanied by ethnic cleansing, which remains in force to this day. Despite having considerable military resources on the island (again, Britain's Cypriot bases are still in business as of 2009) Britain did not act to protect Cypriot independence, remaining as martially passive as it did in the face of Ian Smith's Unilateral Declaration of Independence in the then-Rhodesia. All necessary force in the face of national independence movements, but nothing beyond hand-wringing when confronted by right-wing or reactionary coups was the consistent principle of British imperial governance. [61]

Peaceful decolonisation was not on offer in Aden in the 1960s either. There, a torture centre was set up to deal with liberation fighters where "the standard forms of brutality were employed but, as an official investigation later revealed, more scientific methods of torture were also secretly developed." These included disorientation, electric shocks, hooding, noise, bread-and-water diet and sleep deprivation, all subsequently used at Abu Ghraib. One former soldier explained that he couldn't go into details because of the risk of war crimes prosecutions. [62]

In Palestine, too, the Empire went out fighting. The period of the Mandate, which saw British colonial officials attempt to give effect to the Balfour Declaration's commitment to establish a Jewish national home in the area (a commitment Britain had no conceivable legal right to make), included two Palestinian Arab insurrections. One of these encompassed a 175-day general strike.

These uprisings of the subject people were dealt with by bombing, killing, torture and illegal detention in an attempt to break the resistance to imperialism and to Zionist plans to partition the land. "Bomber" Harris, subsequently famous for ordering the mass bombings of German cities without regard to civilian casualties during the 1939-45 war, advocated "one 250 lb or 500 lb bomb in each village that speaks out of turn." As Newsinger notes, this was the spirit of Guernica abroad, yet unnoticed by democratic Britain at the time. Jenin was virtually blown up by the British in 1938 and 112 Palestinian freedom fighters were hanged (65 years later the Israeli army did much the same thing again to this suffering Palestinian city). Collective punishment was meted out as well – the Arab villagers of Halhul were kept in the open without water for five days, in one example. In the subsequent comment of a Colonial Office official, British rule in Palestine became "purely one of repression." The Palestinian problem and the rest of the Empire's record in the Middle East is considered in more detail in the next chapter. [63]

Nor was violence exclusively directed towards those rising against colonialism with weapons in hand, to nail another myth cultivated by pro-Empire historians. Civilians were often the deliberate targets of the colonialists. Virtually the entire population of Tasmania was exterminated by the Empire in the 19th century. Lord Lugard mounted punitive expeditions in Nigeria "which soldiers seemed to take as a license for lechery as well as butchery." Soldiers raped under-aged girls, finished off the wounded with sporting rifles and removed limbs for the sake of bracelets. Even Churchill was moved to comment that "the whole enterprise is liable to be misrepresented by persons unacquainted with imperial terminology as the murdering of natives and stealing their lands." Lugard's exploits in Uganda (the site of a merciless inter-imperialist struggle pitting Britain against France, all wrapped up in which variety of Christianity was to be imposed on the peaceably pagan Ugandans) were described by the French officer Captain Darcy thus: "Against this helpless, defenceless population Captain Lugard turned his guns and maxims. He exterminated a large number and then, continuing his work of destruction, he gave full rein to his troops and adherents..." Likewise, the pacification of Burma was accomplished by summary execution, looting and flogging. [64]

This violence reached its apotheosis in the institution of the concentration camp, another adornment of twentieth-century imperialist civilisation which was introduced to the world by the British and raised to a more developed pitch by the Nazis. Lord Kitchener – subsequently the War Office poster boy for the First World War – utilised aggressive anti-civilian measures to secure victory in South Africa during the Boer War. This was, in the words of then-Prime Minister Lord Salisbury, displaying the hypocrisy Hitler so admired and the rhetorical flair Tony Blair was to emulate, a "war for democracy", adding that "we seek no goldfields, we seek no territory". The record shows of course, that the British victory in the war left South Africa with no democracy but Britain with control of a lot more territory and gold. [65]

Kitchener's army destroyed 30,000 farms, hundreds of villages and uncounted crops and livestock and drove 160,000 women and children into his specially-constructed concentration camps, where 28,000 died, most of them children. Around a sixth of the Boer population (resisting the incorporation of their states into British-ruled South Africa) died in what the British claimed to be places of refuge. Compounding this crime, British officers sold old wood from a worn-out dance floor to Boer women to make coffins for their children at the price of one shilling and sixpence each. These atrocities did have numerous critics back in Britain – most of them offered more elevated arguments than the creator of Sherlock Holmes, Arthur Conan Doyle, who deplored the British use of dum-dum bullets in the war on the grounds that these "were never intended to be used against white races." [66]

The concentration camps in South Africa were no aberration. After the defeat of the uprising of 1857 80,000 Indian political prisoners were detained and tortured by British army doctors in the "new imperial gulag set up on the hot and impossibly humid Andaman Islands" in William Dalrymple's words, while the huge Hola internment camp in Kenya was the site of extensive abuse, as we have already mentioned. Concentration camps featured in the last years of British rule in Malaya too. [67]

None of these were "extermination camps" of the kind used for the Nazi genocide against Europe's Jews and others. But that cannot acquit the British Empire of genocide. The Aboriginal people of Australia were all but exterminated, and those of Tasmania actually were. Even In New Zealand – supposedly a milder case – the Maori population of about 100,000 in 1840 had been reduced to 42,000 by the end of the century as the colonising population advanced. So in almost every respect the Empire record of violence towards subject people bears the closest comparison to the conduct of the Third Reich.

Enemies of Democracy

Even the most zealous whitewasher of Empire cannot claim that it was democratic in its exercise of power in the colonies, the Raj and the mandated territories. Lord Bentinck, Governor-General of India in 1828-35, outlined the fundamental imperial outlook at an early stage, and at a time when the first serious stirrings of political democracy were being felt in Britain itself. He said that India needed an all-powerful government to protect property. "This is civil liberty," he said. "Political liberty would turn us out of India." [68]

That principle guided the governance of India and the rest of Empire until the end. To take one example, in 1934, when British opinion was waking up to the menace of fascism, the British government in just one colony – Sierra Leone – passed a Sedition Ordinance, an Incitement to Disaffection Ordinance, a Deportation Ordinance and an Undesirable Literature Ordinance. This latter imposed a three-year sentence of imprisonment on anyone possessing books, newspapers or documents which the Governor considered seditious. There seems little to choose between this and Hitler's book-burning. [69]

Of course, there is the oft-repeated boast that the colonies were left with Westminster-style constitutions by the departing colonialists. However, such constitutions were never operational while the British were in place – and nor were they bequeathed until the property question had been secured to London's satisfaction. Indeed, in its last period, British power became more overtly and proactively anti-democratic, intervening to organise the overthrow of elected progressive (and capitalist property-threatening) governments in Iran and in Guyana in the 1950s and to block democratic development in Cyprus, justifying it all to the world by the exigencies of the Cold War.

However, what requires closer inspection is the anti-democratic nature of the imperial project and its protagonists in Britain itself. Empire rallied to itself the most reactionary and authoritarian elements of the ruling class, those who wished to use a global network of colonies and the chauvinistic propaganda which attended its extension to block and where possible roll back any and every democratic development in Britain, restoring at home the unchallengeable rule of property and privilege.

Conversely, the great Empire-builders feared that too much (or any) democracy in Britain would undo their work abroad. Lord Lytton, imperial ruler of India, felt that his countrymen were fast losing the instinct of Empire "because of the spread of democracy" which had left the British with a "deformed and abortive" constitution. He soothed himself by pressing another war of aggression against Afghanistan. [70]

Lytton was not an aberration in his attitudes. The leading imperial proconsuls Lords Curzon and Milner advocated, *inter alia*, the abolition of political parties and parliament. For Milner "an encounter with the electorate as a Liberal candidate in 1885 had given him a distaste for democratic politics which was to grow steadily into contempt for the parliamentary system and its practitioners," according to E.J. Feuchtwanger. [71]

Curzon, when not ruling India or in government, found time to team up with his fellow proconsul Lord Cromer (effective imperial dictator of Egypt for many years) to serve as the chairman and president respectively of the National League for Opposing Woman Suffrage in the 1900s. [72]

So on through the Burke's Peerage of Empire. Lord Meath, the leading promoter of Empire Day as a propaganda tool in Britain before and after the First World War, had a racial mentality and a *sturm-und-drang* outlook fully consistent with fascism: "The survival of the fittest is a doctrine which holds as good in the political and social as in the natural world. If the British race ceases to be worthy of dominion it will cease to rule...Britons have ruled in the past because they were a virile race, brought up to obey, to suffer hardships cheerfully, and to struggle victoriously." These sentiments are noteworthy for the way in which they extend the existing class relationships in Britain onto a world plane, by saying that this is at one and the same time a race destined to rule on the basis of its propensity to obey! Obviously, it was the Lord Meaths who were to be doing the ruling, while the mass of the British people got on with the obeying. [73]

So it is unsurprising that when the Special Branch was set up as Britain's first political police force, it was staffed almost exclusively by men with service in India and Ireland behind them, "which was where its methods were first perfected," according to Bernard Porter. [74]

Not without good cause did C.P. Lucas, a former Colonial Office functionary who later wrote school books from which generations of children learned about the colonies, recommend the Empire as "the most wholesome and effective antidote to democracy." The activities of Lucas and other pro-Empire campaigners also underlines the point made by historian Victor Kiernan that the "culminating stage of imperialism was one of the forcing-houses of modern propaganda, the science of blackening enemies and whitewashing friends." This is a "science" which has since been raised to a considerable pitch of sophistication. When Gordon Brown and George Bush met for dinner with the historian Andrew Roberts as guest in June 2008, it is appropriate that Rupert Murdoch also joined them. [75]

The anti-imperialist campaigner George Padmore had therefore every justification for warning in the 1930s that the colonies were "a breeding-ground for the type of fascist mentality which is being let loose in Europe today." Indeed, Lord Errol openly advocated fascism as the best means of ruling Kenya in the 1930s, where he had secured considerable estates. The colony's governor, Edward Grigg, actually appeared in a blackshirt uniform as a tribute to Mussolini – not such a peculiar move when it is recalled that Winston Churchill had expressed his admiration for the Italian dictator, specifically endorsing his view that possessing colonies was "the measure of national greatness." This entwining of imperialism abroad and fascism at home reached its post-war apogee in France, where the determination of the colonial elite to hold on to Algeria by whatever means of ferocious repression were required led to the collapse of the Fourth Republic and to serious attempts at a fascist takeover in Paris, the danger not abating until Algeria secured its independence. The same forces were at work in Britain in the 1930s. [76]

Eugenics were also popular in the British ruling class (and among Fabian socialists) before World War One. Churchill flirted with the idea in this period, as did John Maynard Keynes, who was vice-president of the English Eugenics Society. None of them would have foreseen that this further imperial "science" was to contribute significantly to the intellectual underpinning of Hitler's extermination campaigns against the disabled and nazi experiments on twins and "inferior races" in the concentration camps – but the "masters of the universe" outlook is unmistakeable. [77]

Niall Ferguson himself strayed into this field in the course of polemics around his book *The War of the World*. Defending himself against the charge of seeking to revive "the racism institutionalised by empire" he asserted that "there is evidence that nature does not favour breeding between genetically different members of a species." There is more to Ferguson than merely his imperial story-telling. [78]

From this we can see, not that all these figures were nazi sympathisers (which some clearly were not) but that, firstly, there is a very intimate connection between imperialist ideas and their ultimate nazi expression, and secondly that even in Britain the pro-imperialist elite was also the most consistent opponent of democracy and the most ardent promoter of chauvinism, racism and male supremacy. It should also serve as a reminder that the impetus towards a right-wing dictatorship in Britain was not confined to fringe figures and groups like Oswald Mosley and his political descendants, but was encamped right at the heart of the Establishment, nourished by the practice and the worldview of imperialism, resting as it does on the authoritarian domination of millions by a self-selected and self-perpetuating elite wrapping themselves in the glory of racial superiority and endless conquest.

Casualties of British Imperialism

Is it possible to compute how many deaths British imperialism has been responsible for? It is certainly not easy. However, it is worth trying. Hitler, Stalin and Mao are currently damned most of all on account of the number of people their regimes killed. In Hitler's case the computation is relatively easy, since all the deaths in World War Two can be laid at this door, at least in respect of the European, African and Middle Eastern theatres. Other powers committed atrocities between 1939 and 1945 and contributed indirectly to the war's outbreak, for sure, but the whole conflict would not have started without

Hitler, whose regime bears in any event a direct responsibility for most of the fifty million casualties, the majority of them civilian. The death tolls attributed to Stalin and Mao, as noted above, depend very largely on how one estimates the famines in the USSR and China.

Numbers killed are not the only measures of a regime of course. It could be widely accepted that it is better to kill one hundred people in a good cause, particularly if that is a necessity for the good cause to triumph, than a single person in a bad one. That logic holds that the British bombing of Hamburg and Dresden, was less of a crime (or even not one at all) than the Nazi attacks on Coventry and London, which cost far fewer lives. The atrocities carried out by those resisting colonialism or fighting for their national independence – and there certainly were such atrocities – cannot, by the same token, be placed on the level with the atrocities carried out by the forces seeking to maintain imperial power.

All that said, it is a measure of a regime currently much-focussed upon, and one that should therefore be applied to colonialism, especially perhaps to the pious and self-congratulatory colonialism of otherwise democratic powers, as much as to any of the other twentieth century systems of government. Of course, as we have already noted, the slave trade alone (the anniversary of the abolition of which in 2007 was greeted with the usual British public self-congratulation as if its existence had been an unfortunate and temporary aberration corrected by a beneficent ruling class as soon as it was drawn to their attention) was Hitlerian in its sweep, consequences and casualty count.

The difficulties in the way of computing a later death toll with any degree of precision, however, are formidable. The main one is that no-one recorded the deaths amongst the indigenous population at the time, in most cases. In other cases the malefactors themselves deliberately destroyed such records as were kept. Many of the crimes of colonialism were carried out in the nineteenth century or earlier, and they were spread out over a much longer period than those of German fascism. We can be fairly exact as to how many people were killed during the Malayan Emergency, for example, but that is a late-Empire exception. So one faces the double difficulty of both assessing numbers and assessing attribution. Clearly, not everyone who died a violent or miserable death in a British colony over a period of a century or more can necessarily have their end blamed on their rulers.

Mark Curtis, writing in his *Unpeople* in 2004, estimates that Britain has "significant responsibility" for between 8.6 and 13.5 million deaths since World War Two and direct responsibility for between 4 and 5.7 million. These figures err on the large side. In the "significant responsibility" list one finds almost every crime committed directly or indirectly by any great power since 1945, including for example the Rwandan massacres or Russia's operations in Chechnya, on the grounds that successive British governments lent some measure of diplomatic or political support to those actually doing the killing. All those 13.5 million people are victims of the imperialist world system but not necessarily British imperialism. However, the reckoning does include the UN-estimated 500,000 – 1 million deaths (mainly children) caused by the Anglo-American sanctions regime against Iraq in the 1990s, and the minimum of 20,000 violent deaths caused by South Africa's apartheid regime. While obviously these deaths are not on the account of the Empire as such, Britain does bear a special responsibility in both cases.

Curtis's list asserting direct responsibility is more robust for our purposes. All the entries do include a measure of direct British responsibility. However, the inclusion of the Vietnam War seems a stretch, since clearly the main responsibility was American, while to attribute all the Korean War deaths to Britain also seems to exaggerate the undoubted co-responsibility of the U.K. for that conflict. Without counting deaths twice, this method would leave the casualty count attributable to the USA post-war at an artificially-low level. On the other hand, Curtis could not in 2004 fully reflect the horrific casualties caused by the occupation of Iraq and, to a lesser extent, Afghanistan, this century. Taking all these factors together, one could attribute between 1.5 and 3 million deaths since 1945 to military or economic warfare undertaken either by Britain or by the US and Britain acting together in harness. Obviously, this does not attempt to address the very much larger number of premature deaths caused in the Third World by the imposition of neo-colonial economic policies. [79]

Of course, that figure does not even begin to scratch the surface. By 1945 the Empire was already in retreat. Kenya, Cyprus and Malaya aside, its worst was generally behind it. To go back further, to the halcyon century of Empire up to World War Two accentuates the difficulties of accurate estimation. As noted above, there are famines in at least two countries which must be added to the record – that in Ireland in 1845-6, and those in India in the late nineteenth century and down to 1943. These famines were rooted in the imposition of an economic way of life designed to serve the needs of British-centred exploitation and social control, and were compounded by incompetence and even indifference on the part of the imperial authorities. The deaths were not actively willed by the British, it could be argued, and therefore belong in a different category. But for the sake of applying with, in our view, more justice the standards used by critics of communism on this point, they should be counted. There is no doubt that they were all human victims of somebody. These famines account for perhaps 30 million deaths by starvation and related diseases – mostly in India, although the blow to Ireland proportionate to population may even have been greater.

Deaths by violent repression, either of those fighting in arms to achieve national liberation, or those simply peacefully asserting their rights, or merely getting in the way of the authorities or settlers, or even just for the sake of collective punishment and the spreading of terror, are harder to compute the further back into the history of Empire one travels. Generally accepted counts for deaths in Aden are at around 1,000. The figure in Kenya during the 1950s is certainly far higher, with 130,000 as a middling estimate. Historians are fairly certain of 10,000 deaths in Malaya during the "emergency", both those killed in action and those executed. A larger number were killed by British troops helping France and the Netherlands re-establish colonial control over Vietnam and Indonesia respectively, perhaps as many as 50,000. 15,000 were killed in the massacre at Surabaya in Indonesia alone, described in more detail below.

Iraq has suffered particularly grievously. Not far short of 100,000 were killed during the 1920s with the imposition of the British "mandate" on the country. Far greater numbers have been killed more recently, of course, in the Gulf War of 1991, the subsequent sanctions regime noted above, and the present continuing conflict. A smaller number – perhaps "only" a few thousand – were dispatched by Britain's repressive rule in the parallel mandate in Palestine.

Further back, one is driven to guess-work. Certainly, coercion (hangings, shootings etc) could easily account for 100,000 deaths in India in the immediate aftermath of the great rebellion alone. Taking the period of the Raj as a whole, the total must be far greater. The figure for Ireland will run to tens of thousands at least, including successive waves of state violence culminating in the operation of the notorious "black-and-tans" after the First World War. How many Chinese died in the various "opium wars" and subsequent British intervention? Hundreds of thousands at least. Likewise in Jamaica in the waves of violence which shackled it to Empire both before and after the abolition of the slave trade. Aboriginal peoples in Australasia were slaughtered in their uncounted tens of thousands, to the threshold of complete extermination. Nor should the imperial massacres in Sri Lanka (Ceylon) be overlooked – the unfortunate country passed from Portuguese to Dutch to British rule, with each in turn leaving a brutal and bloody stamp on the island. [80]

The calculations for Africa are the most imponderable of all. The violence and deliberate economic disruption which accompanied colonialism everywhere from the Cape to Nigeria and the Sudan did not count its victims. It was in Africa that the racism was at its most uninhibited. It would seem that the British carried out no operations as genocidally comprehensive as those unleashed by King Leopold in the Congo and the Germans in Namibia, both of which we briefly examine below. However, Lord Lugard's rule in Nigeria was scarcely a massive improvement, and the brutality of what became the apartheid regime in South Africa was initially baked in under British supervision. Tens of thousands were killed in wars in Sierra Leone. In Africa, aggregated, the number of victims over the whole period of British rule seems more likely to run into seven figures. But it is a statement in itself that we do not really know, even though this covers a period in which every violent death in the United Kingdom itself would be scrupulously accounted for.

So if the question is to be taken as seriously as it deserves, it cannot realistically be answered with any accuracy comparable to that which we can apply to the Nazi dictatorship. However the total, particularly if the famine deaths are included, must leave the British Empire running Hitler very close – over a much longer period certainly, but extending over almost every corner of the globe, including places the Nazis never dreamed of visiting.

Naturally, if one regards the British Empire as a good thing, or even, like Ferguson, an inevitable thing, removed from the scope of moral judgement, then it could be argued that this collateral damage was unfortunate, but ultimately all for the best. The tasty imperial omelette could not be made while leaving all the indigenous eggs unbroken. The view argued here, however, is that the whole enterprise was no more legitimate than the drive by German imperialism for European and perhaps global domination from 1939 onwards.

Far more could, of course, be written on the subject of British imperialism. But the foregoing may at least help to explain why the idea of its revival has so few supporters around the wide world outside of official London and Washington and its media and academic outriders.

The passage with which British historians of the empire in Asia Christopher Bayly and Tim Harper sum up the colonial experience of Malaya could stand duty for the whole of the experience, erring perhaps only in the mildness of the judgement: "The maladministration and graft of the military administration; the wild and unchecked fury of white terror in the first years; the extra-judicial killings of young men and women; the grotesque atrocity exhibitions of the mutilated slain; the violence to family life and livelihoods of hundreds and thousands of farmers and labourers during resettlement; the insidious small tyrannies of a vast and largely unaccountable bureaucracy; the racism and arrogance of empire – all this must be set in the balance." [81]

So it should. But instead Gordon Brown, as of 2009 British Prime Minister, believes it is time Britain stopped saying sorry for the Empire. In 2005 he told the *Daily Mail*: "The days of Britain having to apologise for its colonial history are over. We should move forward. We should celebrate much of our past rather than apologise for it." [82]

The truth is Britain has never started apologising for the record of massacre, exploitation and despoliation that we have only sketched here. Today one is far more likely to hear arguments for starting the whole imperial show up again.

All Empires Together

So much for British imperialism. The record of other European colonial powers was no different and to understand how the imperial question is viewed by most of the nations and peoples of the world it is useful to briefly consider it, the more so since Britain itself was as often engaged in propping up other colonial empires (particularly after 1945) as it was in trying to undermine them. Against the peoples of the South, the great empires maintained an essential solidarity.

King Leopold of the Belgians took second place to no-one in his commitment to the highest moral purposes of imperialism. "The aim of all of us...is to regenerate, materially and morally, races whose degradation and misfortune it is hard to realise," he said. [83]

The King set about this great work of regeneration by inveigling the major colonial powers into allowing him to take over the vast territory of the Congo as his personal property. Casting about for the indispensable ethical justification, he settled on the need to combat slave trading in the region. Under this edifying cover, his rule led to a generation of plunder and genocide extreme even by the general standards of imperialism in Africa. A contemporary academic estimate is that between 1880 and 1920 the population of the Congo was reduced by "at least a half" – a figure of around ten million dead through murder and deliberate starvation to be laid at the door of Belgium and its monarch, who looted the natural wealth of the country in order to amass a vast personal fortune. Of all the barbaric episodes in colonial history, this is one where the comparison to the Nazi holocaust appears most apt. [84]

Ultimately, the other great powers were moved to protest after press exposure of King Leopold's grotesque misrule. The British consul in the Congo in 1908 asked "... what benefits these people have gained from the boasted civilisation of the Free State. One looks in vain from any attempt to benefit them or to recompense them in any way for the enormous wealth which they are helping to put into the Treasury of the State. Their native industries are being destroyed, their freedom has been taken from them, and their numbers are decreasing." All this finally prompted the Belgian government to assume a more conventional direct control of the colony. However, this led to scant improvement in the "degradation and misfortune" of the Congolese people, who were eventually abandoned in haste by their "mother country" in 1960 with scarcely a doctor or a teacher to their name – an extreme example of the general consequence of discriminatory colonial legislation aimed at inhibiting the emergence of indigenous professionals. Belgian colonialism was also gifted Rwanda and Burundi, previously German possessions, after World War One in order to compensate Belgium for the destruction it had suffered at the hands of the Kaiser's army. Thus the precedent of compensating one set of Europeans for the crimes of other Europeans at the expense of the colonial people was established, a precedent later followed in Palestine. Belgium misgovernment, relying as ever on divide-and-rule, this time between Hutu and Tutsi, helped prepare the way for the genocide in Rwanda in the 1990s.[85]

But Leopold and the Belgians were not uniquely awful colonialists – or the awfulness was only a matter of degree. The British Foreign Office acknowledged at the height of the international controversy about Leopold's genocidal plundering that there was almost "no atrocity in the Congo – except mutilation – which cannot be matched in our Protectorate" of Kenya – a country of "nigger- and game-shooters" according to one official. [86]

Nor was this comparison drawn solely in relation to Kenya. British punitive expeditions in the Sudan after World War One were described by one District Officer as "regular Congo atrocities." These involved using the RAF as well as ground troops "since the RAF wanted to test the 'moral effects' of bombing and strafing in an ideal proving ground." If King Leopold became the pre-Nazi gold standard for colonial atrocity, then it was one many contemporary observers saw the British as being within sight of attaining. [87]

Germany's own history of genocide did not start with Hitler. "If Germany is to become a colonising power, than all I say is 'God speed her!' She becomes our ally and partner in the execution of the great purposes of Providence for the advantage of mankind" – thus the grand old man of liberal imperialism William Gladstone to the House of Commons in 1885. [88]

And what an ally and partner Germany proved to be! Her principal colonial acquisitions were in Africa, and included the territory that is now Namibia. This rule was marked by an extreme genocidal brutality which makes it clear that Nazism did not suddenly emerge out of a clear Prussian sky. The main contribution of German colonialism was not the "execution of the great purposes of Providence" but rather the execution of the Herero people in Namibia, almost to the last man, woman and child.

In language that strikingly anticipates later German imperialist rhetoric, the colonial authorities set themselves the task of "the settlement of the Herero problem," the essence of which "was to deprive the Herero gradually of their land and cattle, in other words their means of subsistence." This cynical and callous policy, designed to clear space for German settlers, in the end produced the inevitable uprising.

German military strategy to counter the uprising was to drive the Herero into the desert, and away from their last watering hole. This was successfully accomplished. "As a result, the great majority of the Herero met a slow, agonising death," in the words of one German historian. In three years, by these policies, 65,000 (out of 80,000) Herero were killed, and more than 10,000 Nama (out of 20,000). The Germans killed one-third of a further people, the Damara, simply because they were unable to distinguish them from the Herero. [89]

This was too much even for the son of Jan Christian Smuts, who remarked: "The German idea of colonisation was…extermination," and not just "straightforward extermination, but sadistic ill-treatment, flogging, interference with women and brutality." [90]

But it was not too much for British Conservatism. Despite this record, the British imperial elite was quite prepared to turn large chunks of Africa over to the tender mercies of the still more virulently brutal Nazis in the 1930s. In a little-remembered aspect of appeasement, Neville Chamberlain was willing to offer Hitler a motley collection of African territory (at the expense of other colonial powers like Portugal and Belgium in many cases, in the traditional British way) to compensate for the removal of Namibia, Tanganyika and other colonies from German control into the "trusteeship" of Britain or South Africa after World War One. The plan foundered not on any consideration of the likely consequences for black Africans from being surrendered to the overt and violent racism of the Nazis, but because Hitler was uninterested in making the reciprocal policy concessions to limit his ambitions in Europe which Chamberlain required. Even in September 1939, the British government did not rule out restoring colonies to Hitler – if only he would foreswear violence against European states! [91]

No European power can be acquitted. Up to a million Algerians are estimated to have died during their national war of independence from France. Indeed, on the very day that Europe was celebrating the defeat of fascism in May 1945, 45,000 Algerians were being massacred at Setif, Guelma and elsewhere by the French, the latter's armed forces displaying a martial vigour against unarmed demonstrators largely missing when they confronted armed Germans in 1940. The same month, French colonialism killed up to 2,000 people in Damascus as it re-established its grip on Syria. And the French also slaughtered no fewer than 80,000 Madagascans in the late 1940s. In all cases, France asserted its power through methods in no sense readily distinguishable from fascism. French President Nicolas Sarkozy's assertion that "France has always stood for human rights, while never having committed crimes against humanity" would, as Anatol Lieven has pointed out, "come as a very considerable surprise to France's former colonial subjects." [92]

French rule in Indochina and Dutch rule in Indonesia were similarly bloody in their establishment, maintenance and liquidation alike. Here Britain bears a particular responsibility, since British forces were widely deployed after the defeat of Japan in an effort to re-establish European colonial domination throughout the region, and not just in those colonies which had been British-controlled before the successful Japanese offensive of 1942. As during the Boxer Rising of 1901 in Beijing, the European elite stood united against the indigenous population and their demand for national independence. British forces, using defeated Japanese troops as auxiliaries, helped restore the power of the French colonialists (who conducted themselves with 'maximum ineptitude and considerable cruelty' in Labour MP Tom Driberg's estimation) in Vietnam, thereby setting the fuse for thirty years of catastrophic war which saw the Vietnamese ultimately see off Japanese, British, French and US occupiers. [93]

In the course of hoisting the Dutch back into the saddle in Indonesia (where they remained for only a further three years), British troops killed between ten and fifteen thousand people in the city of Surabaya. This was a vindictive and savage reprisal operation for the assassination of a British general in the course of pro-independence disturbances in the city. Surabaya is all but unique in the annals of British colonial violence in that it actually led to an apology from the British government, albeit not until 2001. [94]

Even the perennially dysfunctional Italian state made its contribution to this roll of shame, its invasion of Ethiopia (Abyssinia) in 1935 being accompanied by the customary extermination of native peoples in their own lands. Learning from the British example in Iraq, weapons of mass destruction in the form of over 300 tonnes of chemicals munitions were dropped on the unfortunate Ethiopians, of whom more than 300,000 perished during the war. Before the installation of Mussolini's fascist regime Italian colonialism had already distinguished itself by deporting to the desolate Tremiti Islands hundreds of Libyan families who had objected to the arrival of Italian interlopers. There they were abandoned to their fate (mainly death through disease and malnutrition) and a precedent set to be followed, in a milder form, in anti-immigrant operations by John Howard's Australian government nearly a century later. Under Italian rule Libya's native population fell from 1.4 million in 1907 to 825,000 in 1933, as a result of near-genocidal colonial policies. "Italians in their Empire killed as much because they were European imperialists as because they were fascists" writes RJB Bosworth in words which have more general application. [95]

The foregoing makes no claim to be a definitive accounting of the record of the European empires. A full reckoning of the massacres, exploitation and other calamities visited on most of the world by colonialism would require a much longer book. And imperialism is not just about mass killing. That can ebb and flow and there are periods and places in which colonial rule was relatively peaceful. It is above all the denial of the right to self-determination, a collective mutilation of people's aspirations. It is not just the taking of lives, it is the controlling and ultimately warping of the lives of hundreds of millions in a power relationship, essentially a racist despotism, that was and is at the heart of empire.

All this is hopefully sufficient to indicate why the question of a revival of imperialism is regarded so differently in Asia, Africa, Latin America and the Middle East than it is among the coterie of pro-Empire historians and pamphleteers in London and Washington; to underline that Hitler was far from unique in his evil; and that the claims of Britain and the other great powers to be "exporting civilisation" is bound to be regarded with near-universal scepticism. Far from enough time has passed for these crimes to be considered expiated. Unlike the nazi regime, British imperialism still lives.

And if anyone thinks the interweaving between Nazism and colonialism is overdrawn, consider one final anecdote, taken from *Time* magazine in 1947 (two years after France had been liberated from Hitlerite occupation and as it was trying to reestablish its own rule in Vietnam), which needs no additional commentary:

"A good part of the French Foreign Legion fighting against the Vietnamese in Indo-China is made up of former members of the Nazis' Afrika Corps. Last week at Hia Duong, the French executed two of their German soldiers for desertion. Before death struck, each procliamed his final faith in a defiant shout. "Vive la France!" cried one. "Heil Hitler!" cried the other." [96]

Chapter Three
Why "They" hate "Us"

"WHY DO they hate us?" US citizens asked plaintively after the 9/11 attacks. "Because they have a grievance culture" came the establishment answer. How convenient – the world's Muslims as sulky adolescents.

Still more self-satisfied is the popular assertion that "they hate us because of our freedom and prosperity," as if there could be no other conceivable reason for Muslims around the world to have issues with the US government. Obviously, it suits the authors of the "long war" to assert that they are facing an irreconcilable and irrational enemy in political Islam, which draws no mobilising strength from the policies followed by the USA and Britain but is instead rooted in a hatred of Western society, culture and values.

Tony Blair expressed a variant of this view in a major speech in 2006:

"... by the early 20th century, after renaissance, reformation and enlightenment had swept over the Western world, the Muslim and Arab world was uncertain, insecure and on the defensive. Some countries like Turkey went for a muscular move to secularism. Others found themselves caught between colonisation, nascent nationalism, political oppression and religious radicalism. Muslims began to see the sorry state of Muslim countries as symptomatic of the sorry state of Islam. Political radicals became religious radicals and vice versa. Those in power tried to accommodate the resurgent Islamic radicalism by incorporating some of its leaders and some of its ideology. The result was nearly always disastrous. The religious radicalism was made respectable; the political radicalism suppressed and so in the minds of many, the cause of the two came together to symbolise the need for change. So many came to believe that the way of restoring the confidence and stability of Islam was the combination of religious extremism and populist politics." [1]

As an explanation for what has happened to the Arab and Muslim worlds over the last one hundred years this was breathtaking in its omissions. Here is a partial list of what the then-premier overlooked:

The colonisation of much of the region by the British and French after the (assisted) disintegration of the Ottoman Empire leading to the arbitrary partition and redivision of territories; the Balfour declaration lending British support to Zionism; the first British occupation of Iraq, fortified by the use of chemical munitions against civilians; the US guarantee to the House of Saud to maintain it in power as long as it provided cheap oil in return; the overthrow of the progressive and democratically-elected nationalist regime of Mossadeq in Iran by MI6 and the CIA; the prolonged and bloody attempts of French colonialism to maintain its power in Algeria; the Suez invasion of Egypt in 1956; the effective underwriting of the Israeli occupation of the West Bank for nearly forty years; "counter-insurgency" in Aden; the support afforded to any despot prepared to massacre the secular and democratic left in his own country and keep petrol at a price which keeps Cadillacs on the road in California; the unstinting assistance afforded to the Shah of Iran's dictatorship right to its very end; the indulgence shown to terrorism as long as it was anti-Communist in Afghanistan.

Tony Blair missed all of this in his historical excursus, apart from a passing and passive reference to "colonisation," which gets equal billing with nationalism – akin to saying that in 1940 Britain was "caught" between democracy and Nazism. This historical head-in-the-sand routine was perhaps no surprise – during the 1997 General Election campaign Blair had to be talked out of saying how proud he was of the British Empire by Robin Cook. [2]

And the history he traduced is still alive and kicking – the consequences of it shape almost every aspect of the contemporary Arab and Muslim worlds. Few Muslims sign up to the Blair view of it. Far more actually attribute the "sorry state of their countries" to the aggressive imposition on them of the priorities of imperialism, along with rulers compliant in delivering those priorities. The vast majority of Muslims in the world come from countries in a great arc from Morocco to Indonesia which have without exception been colonies or semi-colonies well within living memory, whose peoples have been oppressed and their countries exploited. It is true that they have suffered not because they were Muslim but because they were in the way, sitting on top of desirable resources, or simply making a nuisance of themselves. However, neither should it be ignored that Muslim-baiting formed part of the racist political repertoire of the empires, British included, from an early stage. The great uprising in India of 1857, for example, was an enterprise in which Hindus and Muslims participated equally and in unity. This did not stop Raj justice afterwards portraying the whole affair as a dastardly plot by the adherents of a misbegotten "Mohammedan" faith. In William Dalrymple's words, the episode became part of a "global Muslim conspiracy with an appealingly visible and captive hate figure at its centre *[the Mughal of Delhi – AM]*, towards whom righteous vengeance could now be directed." It all sounds very familiar.[3]

Likewise, it should be stressed that the "war on terror" is not, however, a "war on Islam", despite plausible appearances. It has in fact potentially been a war on everyone – or at least anyone who gets between the US elite and its objectives. The US has attacked Vietnam, Nicaragua, Panama, Yugoslavia and Grenada, to name some of its non-Muslim targets over the last generation or so, and presently threatens Cuba, North Korea and Venezuela inter a considerable amount of alia. The devouring dollar knows no religion. But this war does bear exceptionally hard on Muslim countries at the moment. To ask Muslim community leaders to tackle "extremism" effectively when every night you can see on television a Muslim child being pulled lifeless from the rubble caused by the operations of the bloc of the USA, Britain, Israel and other white settler states like Canada and Australia (the exact military division of labour varying from one theatre of war to another) is asking a lot. When the next item may well be the Prime Minister or the President saying, "let the killing continue," then it is raising the bar very high indeed.

A serious study of Muslim opinion in 2008 highlighted the self-serving evasions in the Blair view of the world. A Gallup survey of tens of thousands of Muslims in 35 different countries across the world showed that the adherents of the Islamic religion are perfectly capable of discriminating between one Western country and another. For example, 75 per cent of Egyptians in the survey have an unfavourable view of the US, but only 20 per cent regard France that way. Two-thirds of Kuwaitis are also critical of the US, while only three per cent are critical of Canada. 45 per cent of Lebanese Muslims see the British government as "aggressive" while, unsurprisingly fewer than ten per cent take that view of either Germany or the former colonial power, France. [4]

France is, of course, as much a part of Western civilisation as the USA, and Germany is as Christian as Britain. Politics, not religion, is shaping Arab and Muslim views of Anglo-American conduct. This should not have been news.

"Blowback" not "Bollocks"

And indeed it wasn't to those studying the matter more closely. Shortly after the attacks on London's transport system in July 2005, the blue-chip Royal Institute for International Affairs published a briefing entitled *Security, Terrorism and the UK*. A key problem in tackling terrorism, the authors observed, "is that the UK government has been conducting counter-terrorism policy 'shoulder to shoulder' with the US, not in the sense of being an equal decision-maker, but rather as pillion passenger compelled to leave the steering to the ally in the driving seat." [5]

This has now become more widely understood. The British-born authors of the atrocity and, as far as one can tell, those subsequently arrested for plotting similar attempts, all seem to have been protesting against British foreign policy. In and of itself, that does not make that foreign policy wrong, certainly it does not make bombings and like attacks right. But it is purely absurd to deny that link and pretend that the attackers were motivated by something else – specifically, some malignancy lurking in the heart of their religion, a formulation which could be, and was, used to whip up anger and fear against the totality of the Muslim community in Britain. Tony Blair had, of course, good reason for denying the connection between his policies and terrorism. Were it to be admitted, then his last justification for the Iraq War – that it was about "making Britain safer from terrorism" – would not only be shown to be wrong, but in fact the exact reverse of the truth. It was not until 2009 that Lord West, the British government's counter-terrorism adviser finally abandoned the unequal struggle against cause-and-effect and inelegantly described Blair's view that Muslim disaffection in Britain had nothing to do with foreign policy as "bollocks."

US policy towards Afghanistan is a case study in the dialectics of "blowback." With what now looks like reckless abandon, the US mobilised, organised, funded and equipped a multinational force of radical Islamists in order to give the USSR its own "Vietnam" in Afghanistan. Here Osama bin Laden first came to prominence, and started laying the foundation for al-Qaida as the instrument of his radical agenda. But what were a few "crazed Muslims" compared to the great goal of bringing down Soviet power asked Zbigniew Brezezinski who, when Jimmy Carter's national security adviser, had gone to the Hindu Kush to flamboyantly urge Osama's army onwards against godless communism. Perhaps even now he still holds that view, but it would be fair to assume that many U.S. citizens do not. [6]

But with the hammer-and-sickle not merely expelled from Afghanistan but hauled down from the Kremlin itself, bin Laden moved on. For while the infidel, in its Communist form, had been driven out of one Muslim land in Afghanistan, he noticed that it had moved in, wearing US colours during the 1991 Gulf War, on another – Saudi Arabia. Saudi Arabia is not just bin Laden's own homeland but also the site of Islam's holiest places. Removing the alien presence from Saudi Arabia now became his principal objective, and one he devoted his newly-formed network to securing.

So al-Qaida spent the 1990s attacking US diplomatic and military targets around the world. President Clinton responded by blowing up an aspirin factory – in fact the aspirin factory – in the Sudan. That is how matters stood between the Saudi protégé and his former mentors in the USA until 9/11.

The attacks on New York and Washington found bin Laden and his main associates in Afghanistan, whence they had removed after being evicted from Sudan. So it was Afghanistan which bore the brunt of the wrath of the US. It overthrew the Taliban government in Kabul, leading to an occupation and war which continues to this day, with the military and political position of the occupiers deteriorating markedly as time has gone on. Indeed, at the time of writing the conflict is spilling over into Pakistan on a regular basis – the same Pakistan which had its own democracy undermined and its secret services built up and radicalised in the course of the anti-Soviet Afghan war.

So the blowback has blown back and forth, and is far from blown out yet. Where, however, did the wind first rise?

Sykes-Picot and Balfour

America and Australia were "discovered" by Europeans, we were taught in school. There has never been any argument that the Middle East was always there, however, with Bible stories and six crusades to prove it. However, contemporary "Western" involvement in the region can be traced to the years before the First World War as oil was discovered and the ruling power, the Ottoman Empire, started to crumble under pressure from nationalist movements among its subject peoples and from more advanced European states. The slow-motion disintegration of Ottoman power opened the door still wider to freebooting imperialist interference driven by both strategic and economic reasons (including the growing dependence of the Royal Navy, still the main instrument of Empire, on oil). The *coup de grace* fell as a consequence of the Ottoman alliance with Germany during the 1914-1918 war. If ever a state could not afford to be on the losing side, it was the Ottoman. It ended up with the empire reduced to Ataturk's secular state of Turkey.

Strategists in Britain and France had long been planning for this opportunity, in anticipation of the final Ottoman collapse. Britain had started attacking coastal towns on the Arabian peninsula a hundred years earlier. Aden was annexed as a trading port by Britain in 1839. Egypt, which will be dealt with in more detail below, had become a financial and political dependency of London in the last quarter of the nineteenth century. By the twentieth century, policy had become clear and was adumbrated by Lord Crewe: "What we want is not a united Arabia, but a disunited Arabia split into principalities under our suzerainty." [7]

Crewe's plan came to pass under the impact of world war. In 1916 the British and French governments signed the secret Sykes-Picot Agreement, agreeing their spheres of influence in former Ottoman territories. Almost all of the borders agreed by the two imperialist diplomats at that time remain in place today. The intention was that Britain should take control of what is now Jordan, most of Iraq, Kuwait and an area around Haifa, while France was to control south-eastern Turkey, Northern Iraq, Syria and Lebanon. At that time, the intention was to place Palestine under international control but it was allotted to British management instead, with baleful consequences.

When Sykes-Picot became public, it outraged the nascent Arab nationalist movements, which had fought with the British against the Ottomans during the First World War in the hope of securing Arab national independence. But Arab protest barely registered with the great powers. The main points of the Agreement were endorsed and the various mandates – colonies in all but title – were allocated by the League of Nations in 1922. The British mandate over Palestine, an overwhelmingly Arab-inhabited territory, was of the most lasting significance. In 1917, the British government had endorsed the principle of establishing a Jewish homeland in Palestine – the Balfour Declaration – following intensive lobbying by the Zionist (Jewish nationalist) movement. The mandate ratified the Balfour Declaration and therefore gave Britain the responsibility, inter alia, of establishing the national home for the Jewish people on this Arab land.

The Balfour Declaration had also stated that the rights of the Arabs in Palestine were not to be "prejudiced" by British sponsorship of the Zionist project. As has often been said, by this time perfidious Albion had promised the Promised Land to just about everyone. However, it was abundantly clear that the promise to the Arab people of Palestine would be the first to be discarded. Balfour, in a subsequent statement, was quite explicit about this. "We do not propose to go through the form of consulting the wishes of the present inhabitants of the country," he said in 1919, adding that Zionism was "of far profounder import than the desires and prejudices of the 700,000 Arabs who now inhabit that ancient land." [8]

The Tory MP and arch-strategist of colonialism Leopold Amery was likewise clear as to why this had to be so. Palestine was "a central pivot for our whole Middle East policy as well as assuring the effective control of our sea and air communications with the East." Zionism was, at this stage, an instrument in the hands of British imperialism, allowing London to control a strategic strongpoint on the cheap (getting in ahead of French rivals) without offending the rising power of the USA, where Zionist sentiment was already becoming a political factor. Ronald Storr, Governor of Palestine in the 1930s, further gave the game away when he said that "A Jewish state…could be for England 'a little loyal Jewish Ulster' in a sea of potentially hostile Arabism." The disregard for the rights of the Palestinian Arabs (under the Mandate observers were already comparing the relative positions of Arab and Jewish labour in Palestine to that of black and white workers in apartheid South Africa), and their displacement by primarily European settlers over many decades, has led to the most fundamental conflict in the region. It should always be recalled that this enduring crisis was created by and rooted in the policies of the British Empire and its masters. [9]

Things went no better for the peoples in Britain's other newly-acquired Middle Eastern mandate. In 1917, in line with the secret provisions of Sykes-Picot, British troops invaded Mesopotamia, which comprises much of modern Iraq. These lands had been part of the Ottoman Empire since the sixteenth century. As Sluglett and Sluglett record "...there was no particular sense in which the three provinces formed a geopolitical or economic unit," unlike Egypt and Syria. The third province – loosely, contemporary Iraqi Kurdistan – was only shifted into the new British-denominated state at Churchill's prodding following the discovery of the Mosul oilfields. It would otherwise have fallen under French control. As elsewhere in the colonial world, natural unities were split up, while more-or-less arbitrary state units were created elsewhere – although it is sometimes forgotten that Iraq had existed as an entity in more distant history. [10]

London promptly installed a monarchy – under King Faisal – amenable to British control since, in Albert Hourani's assessment, "the ruling group [in Iraq] was small and unstable and had no solid base of social power to rest on." [11]

Britain's bloody role in Iraqi history began at the new country's birth. Iraqi opposition – both Arab and Kurdish – to imperial rule was put down by extensive aerial bombardment – its first use for such a purpose. "To end the Iraqi insurgency of 1920...the British ...relied on a combination of aerial bombardment and punitive village-burning expeditions. Indeed, they had contemplated using mustard gas, though supplies had proved to be unavailable," Niall Ferguson laconically records. 98,000 Iraqi civilians were killed in the course of this campaign, which ironically included bombing the very same areas against which Saddam Hussein used (Western-supplied) chemical munitions in 1988. Only the latter episode is now recalled in Britain. [12]

The RAF's part in this represented something of a tactical breakthrough. Bombing was now seen as "the cheap, efficient, modern method of colonial control," an insight developed to a refined pitch by the USA in particular in more recent times. The RAF took to giving demonstrations of bombing "native villages" at the Hendon air show, showing off the devastating effect it had on primitive Arab housing. The RAF did acknowledge that this meant that "we rely on 'frightfulness' in a more or less severe form." Winston Churchill, the main imperial architect of the new Iraq, was nevertheless "strongly in favour of using poisonous gases against uncivilised tribes." How many Guernicas were destroyed across Iraq in these years, now unremembered because the victims were colonial, not European, and the perpetrators British, not German? [13]

The extent of Iraq's oil fields became fully appreciated in the mid-1920s, with the main commercial interests held by Royal Dutch/Shell, Anglo-Persian (better known as BP), the French state company CFP, and various US enterprises. In 1928, those partners endorsed the so-called Red Line Agreement, which committed them to cooperate on all oil operations within the former Ottoman Empire. Iraq achieved formal independence in 1932, although Britain remained entirely dominant, through the retention of military bases and transit rights for British forces, among other levers.

The monarchy was ousted in 1939, but in 1941 British forces invaded and occupied Iraq, concerned that the pro-German Arab nationalist Prime Minister Rashid Ali might cut off oil supplies. The British hoisted the King back onto his throne and remained the real power (an authoritarian and exploitative one at that) until the revolution of 1958. The consequences of British rule lay mainly in perpetuating Iraq's social and economic backwardness, relying on a landlord class which, as Sluglett records, "consumed rather than invested and played an essentially parasitic role in the economy while bearing down heavily in the peasantry. It is important to stress that these tendencies were the direct result of British policies during the Mandate and…had been elaborated at the time in order to produce this overall result." [14]

Enter the USA

Whilst Britain and France had longstanding colonial involvement in the Middle East, and a dominant interest in its oil resources, the US emerged in the post-war years as a major rival. Although Washington had initially wanted the UK to maintain its military role in the region for the greater pan-imperial good, its own oil interests quickly trumped that policy. Oil was understood, in the emerging Cold War context, to be more than ever a matter of strategic economic security. The US rapidly developed a substantial thirst for Middle Eastern oil in particular. Before 1939 it had more than met its own requirements with new oil discoveries within the homeland coming thick and fast. But by 1943, senior figures in the Roosevelt administration were coming to the conclusion that domestic production would no longer meet demand. Indeed, by 1948 the US was a net importer of oil. The imperial logic was that the US had to control and develop foreign oil reserves, in order to conserve its domestic supplies and ensure energy security. The Middle East was the obvious location of these reserves, and Saudi Arabia was the key focus for US interest. An investigative trip in 1943 declared that "the oil in this region is the greatest single prize in all history." [15]

However, the self-same oil was also lusted after by another foreign power. Britain had dominated the Middle Eastern oil industry since World War One, and it strenuously attempted to maintain that control into the post-war world. US intentions sparked outrage and anxiety in official London, notwithstanding the wartime "special relationship" Lord Beaverbrook – imperial newspaper baron and adviser to Churchill – urged the premier to refuse to share Arab oil with the US at all. The realities of power did not permit such an intransigent stand, however, and eventually President Roosevelt offered Churchill a carve-up: Persian (Iranian) oil for the British, joint control of Iraqi and Kuwaiti reserves, but Saudi oil to be reserved for the US alone.

Sharing the oil with the Arab peoples themselves did not seem to have occurred to anyone (including, it must be said, the Arabs' own pliant imperial-sponsored rulers). For many years the peoples of the region were regarded as an unavoidable nuisance – natives inconsiderate enough to live atop "our" oil. However, the amicable agreement on the disposition of resources between the great powers did not last long – such deals seldom do. The US oil companies wanted to expand beyond the bounds set down by Roosevelt and Churchill. Some features of the status quo assisted these aspirations, British corporate greed among them. Britain's exploitation of Middle Eastern natural resources was extreme – paying only 10-12% royalties to local governments. This gave the US an easy bargaining chip to use against their British rivals , as it set about displacing them from their pre-eminent role in the region and its oil industry.

In reality, the disparity in power between the two imperial states was now so enormous that Britain stood little chance in the contest – London was struggling to hold its Empire together amid a post-war financial crisis, while the US was embarked on its open march towards world domination, reluctantly stopping only at the frontiers of Soviet influence. In the Middle East, the US pursued two objectives – replacing the British as the dominant economic and political power, and suppressing any radicalism that had even the slightest taint (or alleged taint) of communism. The next ten or fifteen years saw Britain systematically displaced from one position of power after another across the region.

The Suez Watershed

In 1952 the pro-British King Farouk of Egypt was finally dispatched from his throne and replaced by nationalist army officers headed by Abdel Gamal Nasser. This was the culmination of a long-developing movement of the Egyptian people against British domination.

As the Ottoman Empire had weakened, Egypt had slipped from its control into the hands of the City of London. Britain took actual control of Egypt's government in 1882 via the management of the country's finances, whilst Egypt formally remained part of the Ottoman territories. Neo-colonial interference in Egypt proceeded along the familiar lines under the proconsul Lord Cromer, whose views we have already encountered. The great hero of Empire General Gordon was involved in repressing local opposition, but nevertheless had a clarity of insight which exactly anticipates today's arguments over the armed resistance to the occupation of Iraq. "They pretend only Mustapha is resisting," he wrote, "whereas the whole nation is backing him up. What right do we have to make ourselves guardians of Egypt…The people do not want us." [16]

As time went on, the people wanted the British less and less. Egyptian nationalism was powerfully-stimulated by the Dinshawai incident of 1906, when collective punishment including hangings and floggings were meted out to villagers after a scuffle arising from a shooting-party of British officers who, while aiming for pigeons in the course of an unauthorised hunt on the villagers land, actually shot a local woman instead. [17]

When Britain went to war with Germany's Ottoman ally in 1914 it declared a protectorate over Egypt, but the strong nationalist movement secured formal independence in 1922. This independence was very formal indeed. Britain retained the Suez Canal and the right to maintain 10,000 troops in Egypt to protect it. This continued military intervention in the country – and the influence that Britain had through Egypt's corrupt constitutional monarchy – meant that anti-British feeling remained strong down to the next world war, when the country was once again a stage for great power conflict to be played out. As Tariq Ali writes "…if the German and Italian armies had defeated the British and entered Alexandria there is little doubt they would have been welcomed as 'liberators' by the nationalist crowd." [18]

This anti-British sentiment culminated in 1952 in the overthrow of the monarchy by a group of radical army officers, known as the Free Officers Movement, under the leadership of Nasser, who became President of Egypt in 1954. The full independence of Egypt from Britain was declared in June 1956 when the last British troops were withdrawn from the Canal Zone.

The next month Nasser nationalised the Suez Canal. The British Empire, acting in concert with France in this case, had always held the canal to be a key strategic asset – in the nineteenth century because it halved the journey time to India, and in the twentieth because it facilitated the transport of oil from the Middle East to world markets. It had become, moreover, a symbol of traditional Western imperial power in the whole region. Thus an act of nationalisation, which in Britain itself might have been regarded even in right-wing circles at the time as no more than irritating state interference in enterprise, became a monstrous assault on the foundations of civilisation when carried out by Egyptians.

Washington was no friend of such nationalisations but it was no friend of formal empires either. It wished to dispatch direct colonialism into history the better to impose a future of imperial control under its own republican auspices. Whilst counselling the increasingly-unhinged British premier Anthony Eden against military intervention over Suez, it stood to be the big winner from the further discrediting of Britain and France as anachronistic colonial powers whose blundering could open the way to communism (Nasser was, indeed, already flirting with the Soviet Union and allied states in response to Western pressure). For the French there was more at stake than just the canal – Nasser's pan-Arabism was destabilising French colonies in North Africa, as Egypt backed the Algerian independence movement in its fight for freedom. Paris was therefore intent upon war, and sought to bring Israel into the war alliance – not very difficult, given Israel's determination not to tolerate any militarily powerful Arab state.

At the end of October 1956, the three powers attacked Egypt. Nasser responded by scuttling ships and blocking the transport of oil supplies through the canal. US President Eisenhower promptly put the boot into Britain and France, refusing to provide them with oil supplies. Britain's economy was also severely weakened by a run on the pound – probably encouraged by the US administration. There was no alternative but to withdraw. The whole episode was a huge humiliation for Britain and France and marked the end of the premiership of Eden, who had compounded his aggression by serial mendacity in the House of Commons and elsewhere about his intentions. The US had pulled the plug on not just this particular colonial adventure but also on the whole British position in the region. Nothing could have made the shift in the global balance of power clearer. British imperial politicians, disoriented by such a stark indication of their diminished status, realised they could not afford to disregard the US position, setting a template for the next fifty years of foreign policy. Despite eventual involvement in the European Union, British diplomacy has since been based upon one principle above all others – being the most loyal partner of the USA in ruling the world. This is a role for which, as Tony Blair observed, a "blood price" must sometimes be paid.

Shah and Ayatollah

The US had shown its willingness to intervene in the Middle East – and to shunt aside the British – even before the Suez crisis. "Blowback" in the region includes a very stiff breeze from Iran. At the start of the twentieth century it was ruled by the Qajar dynasty, which from1906 was a constitutional monarchy. But already Britain was the barely-concealed power behind the scenes. It controlled Iran's oil through the Anglo-Persian Oil Company (BP) from 1905 – Britain's first major source of oil – and launched a political takeover from there. According to Engdahl, "Since 1919, British administrative officials had de facto run the administration of the country to secure this vital monopoly. Niceties of Iranian sovereignty were pushed to one side." In 1921, Reza Khan, a Cossack army officer who assumed the imperial title and reintroduced an autocracy, overthrew the dynasty. Reza Shah, as he became known, set about industrialising Iran under British hegemony, giving British companies favourable tariffs and a protected economic position in the country. In 1941, British and Soviet troops entered Iran to prevent it from allying with the Axis powers and donating its oil to Hitler. Reza Shah, who had grown too friendly with the Nazis, was replaced by his son, Mohammed Reza Pahlavi. [19]

Iran had to work hard after the Second World War to regain even notional national sovereignty – in 1944 *The Times* had suggested a post-war partition of the country between Britain, the Soviet Union and the US. Control of Iran's resources became a major US objective, notwithstanding Roosevelt's earlier division of the spoils with Churchill. The US tried to gain control of the oil industry by offering 50% royalties to the Iranian government in order to trump the greedier British, whose huge oil profits caused enormous local antipathy. But in March 1951 the Iranian Parliament, under the leadership of Mohammed Mossadeq, nationalised the Anglo-Persian oil company, effectively excluding both Britain and the US from the super-profit. In 1953 the two powers put aside their rivalry long enough to cooperate in 'Operation Ajax', a CIA-MI6 operation to overthrow the democratically-elected Iranian government.

Much was made of the supposed "Communist threat" as the usual all-purpose excuse for imperial interference, but in fact Mossadeq – who was a wealthy aristocratic reformer and might have passed as a leading Liberal in Victorian England – drew his political support primarily from the middle class. However, he was dispatched from power and the Tudeh (communist) Party was subject to violent repression and massacre, along with other supporters of the government. The fundamental issue of control over the oil was now resolved in a fashion thoroughly satisfactory to the plotters. The Shah assumed dictatorial powers under US patronage, which he was to wield with sustained brutality, mounting megalomania and unwavering Anglo-American support over the next quarter-century. Under the new settlement, five US oil firms got a 40% stake in the oil industry.

The political consequences of this coup had enormous reverberations. By crushing secular, modernising movements (caught up in a most expansive definition of "the communist menace") such as that around Mossadeq and by backing compliant tyrannies, the US and Britain contributed mightily to the raising of Islamic-inspired movements to the position of chief articulators of popular opposition to imperialism, despite the latter's own sometimes equivocal attitude to the question. Nationalist opposition is now often religious in form – far more so than forty or fifty years ago – but it is rooted in and seeks to address profoundly secular issues. As Nikki Keddie writes, Iran's Islamic revival "...follows a long tradition in both Iran and in the Muslim world of expressing socio-economic and cultural grievances in the only way familiar to most people – a religious idiom arraying the forces of good against the forces of evil and promising to bring justice to the oppressed." Muslim thinkers in the Arab world and beyond "associate Islam with struggles against colonialism and great-power domination." This is often overlooked by secular Western liberals, who end up fetishising religion in their own way, failing to look past the Islamic form of the resistance to see the essence – the actual act of resistance, and the subject of it – behind. [20]

Cheered on from Washington and London, the Shah continued the lop-sided and parasitic development of Iran and the ruthless suppression of all political criticism. Opposition to the despotism was increasingly shaped by religions leaders led by Ayatollah Khomeini, who came to power after a year of anti-Shah protest culminating in the revolution of 1979. On April 1 that year Iran was declared an Islamic Republic with overwhelming popular support. This was a heavy blow to US power in the Middle East, which had used Iran and Israel as its two surrogate powers for commanding the region. [21]

Bring on the Baathists

After the Second World War, US interest in British-dominated Iraq also developed, and for much the same reason – the country's immense oil reserves. In 1958 the pro-British king was overthrown in a popular revolution under the leadership of Abd al-Qassim. The next year a coup attempt against Qassim failed – rising Baathist Saddam Hussein was among the plotters. At this time, the Iraqi Communist Party was the country's largest single political force, able to bring hundreds of thousands of workers and peasants out onto the streets in its support. It is argued that the Communist Party could have taken power in 1958-59 with broad popular support, and controversy continues over its failure to attempt to do so. Destroying the party was a supreme objective of the US, as it had been earlier in Iran, and it was far from loathe to use the Baath, a secular pan-Arab nationalist party with a firm anti-communist orientation established a decade earlier in Iraq and other Arab states, to achieve this objective. [22]

Having survived the 1959 coup attempt, Qassim was confronted with a difficult legacy bequeathed by the British Empire, not least of which was the status of Kuwait. Kuwait had been created out of the Basra province in southern Iraq by the British at the start of the twentieth century, even before its overall assumption of authority in the country twenty years later, taking an oil field and calling it a state. Iraq sought to restore its sovereignty over Kuwait, then as now governed by a biddable kleptocracy, but was prevented from doing so by a mobilisation of British troops. Qassim's response was to move Iraqi diplomacy closer to the Soviet Union. He also undertook a programme of economic reforms funded by oil money –then under the control of the Western-owned Iraq Petroleum Company. It is not hard to guess how such policies went down in Cold War Washington.

In 1963 the Baath and its allies attempted a further coup, this time with full-on US support. Qassim was overthrown, and his downfall was followed by a bloody witch-hunt against Iraq's Communists, an enterprise in which Saddam's party and the CIA worked hand-in-glove. This set the Baath party on the path to undivided control of the country, a situation consummated by means of yet another coup in 1968. At that time Baathism united unbridled authoritarianism with some modernising social policies. This allowed Hussein – soon the regime's *de facto* leader – to build a broader base of support than might subsequently have been credited. He co-opted the punch-drunk Iraqi Communst Party into the government and in 1972 nationalised the Iraq Petroleum Company and seized all foreign businesses. These last initiatives provided the funding for a major extension of education, health and other services and for the emergence of a large middle class which, if not enthusiastic for the regime, at least acquiesced in it for the most part. While the US was not enamoured ofthese reforms, it continued to court Saddam as a possible regional ally, an approach the Iraqi dictator encouraged by banning and hounding the hapless Iraqi Communist Party once more. When the Iraqi dictator launched an invasion of newly-revolutionary Iran in 1980 he had Washington's understanding and, as the bloody conflict dragged on, its active support. Baathism and US Republicanism, not to mention British Toryism, eager arms suppliers to the dictatorship, wrere all pretty much on the same side down to 1990.

Tormenting Afghanistan

The war in Afghanistan since 2001 is only the most recent of a number of British military interventions in that country. None make happy reading. Britain embarked on its first war in Afghanistan in 1839, as it sought to gain control of the region in its contest for influence with Russia. Fighting in 1839-42 and again in 1878-80, Britain secured control of much of the country. Piers Brendon writes that the the puppet ruler installed in 1842, Shah Suja, "could only survive inside a ring of British bayonets. Thus the army of occupation became the common enemy of Afghan tribesmen..." As Shah Suja then, so President Karzai now. [23]

In August 1919, following the third Anglo-Afghan war, Afghanistan won its formal independence. In 1973, the Shah, whose family had ruled the country for two centuries, was overthrown, and a republic introduced headed by Daud. It is often overlooked that the reactionary armed opposition to any form of progress preceded the takeover by the communist People's Democratic Party of Afghanistan in 1978 and had initially been directed against the mildly-modernising regime of Daud. After the 1978 revolution the Carter administration started to fund and train anti-government forces, via the good offices of the Pakistani secret service, with the express purpose, subsequently admitted by Zbigniew Brzezinski, of provoking a debilitating Soviet intervention. In 1979 the Soviet Union did indeed intervene to support the beleaguered government – which Samir Amin has with some justice dubbed "the best period in Afghanistan's modern history" – as it came under increasing attack from the US-backed "holy warriors". This government took the first steps towards social progress in that country, including a radical improvement in the position of women, a popular agrarian reform programme and an expansion of the education system for both sexes. This did it no good with those in the West who were later to choose just those same considerations as the lipstick to adorn the pig of their own military intervention. [24]

Instead, Washington poured huge amounts of money into the war to overturn this secular modernising regime in favour of rule by an alliance of religious reactionaries. In the largest covert operation undertaken throughout the whole history of the Cold War, money, men and materiel were mobilised to defeat the Soviet Union, with the consequences for the people of Afghanistan themselves barely even a secondary consideration.

The country became a magnet for Islamic fighters, 35,000 of whom were recruited from throughout the Muslim world to fight the Soviet troops in an operation co-ordinated by the CIA, the Saudi kleptocracy and the intelligence arm of the Pakistani military regime. Among them was Osama bin Laden, personally chosen by the head of Saudi intelligence to take part. The Soviet army left in 1989 and the PDPA government in Kabul fell three years later (surprisingly outlasting the Soviet government itself). But the forces conjured up by the war did not disappear as fast. Instead, they merely switched targets. Biting the hand that had fed them was next on the holy warriors menu. [25]

In what was now the Islamic Republic of Afghanistan things went from bad to worse. The mujahideen groups fought among themselves in a protracted argument over the spoils of victory until they were displaced by the Taliban, a movement of religious youth under the sponsorship of Pakistani intelligence and educated by Saudi preachers, in 1996. The Taliban drew most of its support from the Pashtuns, the largest ethnic group in Afghanistan. Civil war sputtered on, with the Taliban opposed by a non-Pashtun Northern Alliance. However, by 2001 the Taliban, with Pakistani support, had effective control over most of the country. It imposed an extremely strict interpretation of Islamic law, and the rights of much of the population – including women in particular – were severely curtailed to the point of being abolished. The US and Britain showed no great interest in this development, leaving Afghanistan to stew.

Osama bin Laden was pursuing a more ambitious agenda than the Taliban's – above all driving the foreigners off Saudi soil. His campaign clearly resonated with sections of the downtrodden Saudi population. It embarrassed the ruling family, which owed much of its standing in the Middle East to its role as guardian of Islam's holiest places, and almost all of its protection in power to US support. Squaring this circle was beyond them in the aftermath of the 1991 Gulf War.

Desert Storm

Saddam Hussein, his dystopian regime under mounting strain largely as a result of the disastrous war with Iran which he had provoked with US support, decided to revive the Kuwaiti controversy in spectacular fashion. The dispute between the two dictatorships hinged around the oil-pricing policies of Kuwait and the Gulf states, which were having a very negative impact on Iraq's war-raddled economy. As has already been noted, the view that British-established Kuwait is really Iraqi sovereign territory is quasi-universally held in Iraq, although this position had no standing from the perspective of international law.

There is some evidence that a-nod's-as-good-as-a-wink diplomacy by the US may have encouraged Saddam Hussein to think that it would not respond militarily to an invasion, thus effectively encouraging the despot to run the risk. However, this was a misreading of the intentions of George Bush senior. Once Saddam had overrun his neighbour the US began to put together a coalition for war against its erstwhile ally. The British government was of course joined at the hip to the US in this enterprise, although it had itself been eagerly supplying Iraq with weapons technology and financial credits for years, ignoring such atrocities as Saddam's use of chemical munitions against Iraq's own Kurdish population in 1988. One of the notable features of this war was the dog that did not bark in the night. The Soviet Union of a few years earlier would have been strong enough to have prevented a military "solution" to the crisis, but just a year away from the demise of both Gorbachov's political leadership and the Soviet Union itself, Moscow's decision to endorse the US against Iraq was a clear indicator that the framework of the Cold War was disappearing in the Middle East as elsewhere. The Gulf War was therefore the first major indication of how the US would operate in the sole-superpower world.

War duly followed Iraq's failure to comply with United Nations orders to quit Kuwait, and the sheikdom was rapidly reconquered for the ruling al-Sabah family. Iraq eventually withdrew from Kuwait, its retreating forces being subjected to the horrors of an unrestrained air attack on the road back to Basra. Between 30,000 and 40,000 Iraqis were killed all together. This may have been an easy win for the US, but it was one which begat a number of strategic complications for the victors. Above all, it marked the end of the attempt, heartily supported by sundry Arab monarchies and dictatorships, to build up Iraq as an effective counterweight to the Islamic Republic of Iran, enemy number one in the region. Hedging his bets, Bush ensured that Saddam remained in power in Baghdad, with almost unlimited power to inflict further cruelties on his own people for the next decade (excepting in Iraqi Kurdistan where, under US protection, the worst that happened was a squalid mid-1990s civil war between the region's two political parties, the PUK and the KDP), but no capacity to re-run his Kuwaiti adventure. Washington regarded this as preferable to the most likely alternative Iraqi government – Shia-led and well-disposed towards Iran. In this way, the imperialist solution of 1991 pre-figured its problem of 2003.

As if Saddam's regime were not burden enough, further externally-imposed miseries were heaped on the long-suffering Iraqi people in the intervening twelve years. Economic sanctions were imposed and maintained under Anglo-US pressure, ostensibly to secure Iraqi compliance with UN disarmament resolutions. The sanctions regime was the most comprehensive ever put in place. The consequences were disastrous for ordinary Iraqis, as diseases like polio, typhoid and cholera reappeared in epidemic form, and malnutrition and morbidity increased rapidly. Children suffered disproportionately from the sanctions. According to UNICEF, polluted water, malnutrition, and a shortage of medicines all contributed to a high rate of child mortality. At least half a million Iraqi children died as a consequence of these sanctions, according to UN estimates, something US Secretary of State Madeleine Albright famously declared a "price worth paying."

The outrage at the catastrophic consequences of the sanctions and the failure of international institutions to adequately address the problems led to repercussions in high places from those with a sense of morality and justice. Denis Halliday, who was United Nations Humanitarian Coordinator in Iraq, resigned in October 1998 stating that "we are in the process of destroying an entire society. It is as simple and terrifying as that. It is illegal and immoral." [26]

This destruction of an Arab and Muslim society gave Osama bin Laden the second string to his bow. To the outrage of seeing a major infidel garrison lording it up in Saudi Arabia was added the apparently genocidal sanctions campaign against the people of Iraq.

Post 9/11: Afghanistan and Iraq

The terrorist attacks of 9/11 were directed at reversing these policies and at raising the price for the unconditional support Washington has long given to Israel, notwithstanding the latter's violent repression of the Palestinian people. In fact, however, they opened the gate to a further and catastrophic escalation of US intervention in the region.

Target number one for reprisals was Afghanistan, host to Osama bin Laden and much of the infrastructure supporting al-Qaeda. Bin Laden's earlier services rendered during the anti-Soviet war in Afghanistan and the US oil industry's flirting with the Taliban government in Kabul were both forgotten. Indeed, the Taliban had already lost whatever credit they had, not only as a result of their reactionary obscurantism on almost every point but also by over playing their hand in negotiations over a fuel pipeline planned to cross their territory.

"The Taliban fell out of favour in Washington in July 2001, when U.S.

negotiators proposed conditions for their pipeline," according to William Engdahl. The US representatives told the Taliban leaders, "Either you accept our offer on a carpet of gold, or we bury you under a carpet of bombs." [27]

Bombs it was to be after the attacks on New York and Washington. The US, backed by Britain, launched their strike against Afghanistan in October 2001. At one level this was a success for the US – al-Qaida camps were destroyed and its leadership was killed or dispersed, while the Taliban were removed from power and the Northern Alliance shoe-horned into office in Kabul. However, it is also now clear that nothing was achieved through all this. Thousands of Afghan civilians died as a result of aerial bombardments. Osama bin laden eluded capture and was relatively soon able to recreate much of al-Qaida's infrastructure in Pakistan, while the subsequent invasion of Iraq opened up an entire new theatre of operations and provided him with a host of willing recruits. The new Afghan government under Hamid Karzai, imported from the US for the purpose, proved almost uniquely dysfunctional and corrupt. Real power soon slipped back into the hands of feuding warlords. A mere patina of democracy was retained, and the government's writ contracted to a small area around Kabul. Poverty and hunger became endemic, and heroin production soared once more as the only means of livelihood for many peasant farmers. US and British military operations escalated as a result of this "state failure," with a mounting list of civilian casualties caused by their bombing raids in particular – both in Afghanistan itself and in Pakistan as the conflict widened dangerously in 2008 and 2009. To cap it all, the Afghan government introduced a law legalising rape in marriage among other attacks on women's rights, moving even the occupying powers to protest.

As a result, the Taliban has grown in strength and purpose, feeding off the Karzai regime's failures and a resurgent Pashtun nationalism stimulated by the prolonged foreign occupation. A former British Ambassador to Moscow, Rodric Braithwaite, found on a visit to Afghanistan in 2008 that journalists and professionals, including people working for the occupation itself, were now nostalgic for Mohammad Najibullah, the last Communist leader of the country. "Things were, they said, better under the Soviets. Kabul was secure, women were employed, the Soviets built factories, roads, schools and hospitals, Russian children played safely in the streets. The Russian soldiers fought bravely on the ground like real warriors, instead of killing women and children from the air." Others now praise the Taliban regime for its maintenance of public order, while all are contemptuous of Karzai. As a result, a parade of Western diplomats and soldiers have admitted that there can be no military "solution" to the crisis and that a political process, including engaging the Taliban, will have to be undertaken. Afghanistan stands as a monument to the failed intervention policy of the Washington neo-conservatives and to the limits of 21st century imperialism. [28]

Much of this unfolded while the second George Bush's attention was elsewhere. Afghanistan was never an important strategic target for the Washington neo-cons. Iraq was. The dust was still rising from the ruins of the World Trade Centre when Donald Rumsfeld and other alumni of the Project for a New American Century – which had been urging a regime change war against Saddam on US Presidents for some years – spotted the opportunity to make the transition from policy to practice. That there was not and never had been any evidence connecting Saddam's secular regime with the fundamentalist Islamism of bin Laden and his associates, still less with the 9/11 attacks, was a fact not allowed to stand in the way – the first of many such.

The Bush administration's imperial ambition was to remake the Middle East with a "liberated" Iraq as its fulcrum. The argument of choice was Iraq's alleged possession of "weapons of mass destruction". It is now known that this campaign, in which the US President was ably seconded by Tony Blair, was entirely false. The propaganda around this issue culminated in the infamous claim by the British government that "Iraq's military forces are able to use chemical and biological weapons, with command, control and logistical arrangements in place. The Iraqi military are able to deploy these weapons within 45 minutes of a decision to do so." Saddam had no such weapons, and had not had any for several years at least, a fact that was within sight of being unambiguously verified by the UN weapons inspectors led by Hans Blix who were operating within Iraq in early 2003. [29]

The unfolding of the Iraq War has been exhaustively documented. The conflict, founded upon a falsehood about Saddam's arsenal, proceeded in full violation of international law, a fact apparent to everyone at the time other than Lord Goldsmith, the British government's senior law officer, who gave Blair the green light he required to join in the invasion. As with the Yugoslav War of 1999, the attack lacked any sanction from the United Nations Security Council. France, Germany, Russia, China and India, along with most other states, opposed the aggression. [30]

Nothing deterred, George Bush pushed on and wrote another lurid and bloody chapter in the book of neo-colonial interference in the Arab and Muslim world.

The Iraq War

Operation Shock and Awe was over by May 2003 when Saddam Hussein was driven from power, but the subsequent occupation has been an immense tragedy for Iraq. Estimates suggest that civilian lives lost may be as many as a million (even the Iraqi government itself, with no interest in exaggerating numbers, admitted to more than 150,000 in 2008), infrastructure is devastated, disease, violence and poverty are rife, and – as with the sanctions – children suffer intensely, with high levels of malnutrition reported. Added to this there has been a massive exodus of refugees – more than two million people, or around ten per cent of Iraq's population – leading to severe problems in neighbouring Syria and Jordan. A further two million or so are displaced within Iraq itself. And civil war, based on sectarian divisions sedulously nurtured by the US occupiers, still hangs over the country as of mid-2009, with the short-term effects of the co-option of part of the Sunni resistance by the US wearing off. [31]

Yet there are those who are benefiting from the human catastrophe, and chief among these are those involved in oil. William Engdahl reports a memo from the Oil Depletion Analysis Centre to the U.K. Cabinet Office on September 9th, 2001, which stated, "Global oil supply is currently at political risk…Large investments in Middle East production, if they occur, could raise output, but only to a limited extent. The main exception is Iraq…" [32]

Before the war on Iraq, the Iraqi government had signed long-term oil development deals with Russia, France and China. After the war, the US proceeded rapidly to pay those countries back for their failure to back Bush's war by completely reshaping the Iraqi oil industry. According to Engdahl,

"…as the rubble in Iraq was cleared for oil development in early 2004, Washington declared that oil and reconstruction contracts would go to those who had helped her take Iraq. The first oil companies to reap the benefits were ChevronTexaco, Condi Rice's old company, BP and Shell of the UK, and Cheney's Halliburton." If the oil giants have not harvested their anticipated profits yet, it is only because of nationalist resistance in Iraq to losing control of their greatest economic asset. [33]

US companies also dominated the takings in reconstruction contracts, even though Iraqi companies had experience of just such work after the previous war. Over 150 US companies received contracts worth more than $50 billion in total. Halliburton received the largest at $12 billion, with 13 other companies awarded contracts of over $1.5 billion each. [34]

Subsequent operations have been dogged by corrupt practices, fraud and mismanagement. While the Iraqi people suffer, starve, are brutalised, tortured and killed, the US and its allies have engaged in a massive asset-stripping operation. Indeed, the argument of Ian Boal and others that the Iraq War is part of a "radical, punitive, extra-economic restructuring of the conditions necessary for expanded profitability…as new form of military neoliberalism" is irrefutable in view of the occupation's record. [35]

The US colonial overlord Paul Bremer, during his year in office, ordered the privatisation of 200 state-owned enterprises; imposed a flat rate of tax at 15 per cent, binding on the giant US corporation and the Iraqi labourer alike (thereby fulfilling a neoliberal dream which it has been impossible to realise even in the US itself); removed all restrictions on the export of dividends, profits and investments; scrapped all tariff and custom barriers; and gave foreign companies immunity from Iraq law under certain conditions. Some of these decrees were in flat breach of international law regarding foreign occupations, and many were made binding on post-occupation "sovereign" Iraqi governments. These were, Bremer later said, among his "biggest accomplishments" during his time in Baghdad, displaying an acute sense of the purpose of his mission. As *Washington Post* reporter Rajiv Chandrasekaran states in his illuminating account of the occupation, "Bremer had come to Iraq to build not just a democracy but a free market." No doubt for that reason, the proconsul was careful to leave Saddam's laws radically curtailing trade union rights on the statute books.   If more has not been achieved for the Bush administration's corporate sponsors, it is only because of the violent resistance to the occupation regime by tens of thousands of Iraqis. [36]

This potted history of the insertion of Anglo-American power into the Middle east is very different from the narrative espoused by Tony Blair. It amounts to this – repeated invasion, plunder of resources, the installation of dictatorships and royal autocracies, the suppression of any threatening democratic development, the gift of Arab land to Israel, partition and destabilisation. And the invasion and occupation of Iraq, with its massacres (Haditha), torture (Abu Ghraib) and destruction of cities (Fallujah) has revealed to a new generation that this is not history alone, but the contemporary policy of the great powers and the renewed imperialism.

And that is why "they" hate "us". The only wonder is that they do not hate us more.

Chapter Four
Tony Blair's Victorian values

"...those people will never begin to advance...until they obtain the rights of man; and these they will never obtain except by means of European conquest."
– Winwood Reade, *The Martyrdom of Man*, 1872 [1]

"VICTORIAN VALUES" was a slogan Margaret Thatcher was rather fond off. In this respect, as in others, Tony Blair was her faithful follower. In one respect, he went even further than his predecessor in embracing Victorian standards of public conduct – invading other countries behind a screen of sanctimonious justifications. Working as she did amidst the confines of the Cold War, Mrs Thatcher was perhaps not able to do as much along that line as she would have wished, although to be fair to her she did display some scruples about ignoring international law (even denouncing her friend Ronald Reagan for doing just that when he invaded Grenada). Neither geopolitics nor conscience supplied any such restraint on Blair's uninhibited war mongering.

It was in his role as advocate for the Bush wars that the British Prime Minister raised himself from what would otherwise have been in strictly military terms a bit-part role in the whole enterprise. By supplying liberal, humanitarian and internationalist arguments for the Yugoslav, Afghan and Iraq Wars, Tony Blair played a large part in launching and sustaining the whole enterprises. He was better placed for this work, as an articulate Labour Prime Minister, than was a tongue-tied conservative Republican President.

Thus Blair emerged as the principal avatar of "liberal interventionism": the desirability – indeed, the necessity – of the great Christian powers (he has never accorded any such right to other leading states) invading other countries in ostensible pursuit of the imposition of democracy, human rights and social justice. [2]

One charge that cannot be laid against the former Prime Minister is that this outlook represented a categorical break with the entirety of the liberal and labour tradition in Britain. It did mark a significant departure from the mainstream of post-war social-democratic thought on international relations in its open disregard for United Nations authority and the provisions of international law generally, its neglect of peaceful mediation to settle disputes and its setting aside of the principle of national sovereignty. But in so doing Blair tapped into a current of thought as old as the British Empire – that a little imperialism in the right hands is a good thing not just for the "national interest" or for order in the world but also for the promotion of social improvements amongst the conquered.

This is an important flank in the political controversies around the present wars. Despite the best endeavours of Niall Ferguson, Robert Cooper and the rest to reintroduce Empire into operating political vocabulary, it remains the case that imperialism today still prospers best under a different name. Even in the 19th century, when Empire could be advocated without linguistic acrobatics, colonialism was still nevertheless often dressed up as something else, an act of philanthropy or even piety, certainly something conducted for the good of the conquered, of civilisation or humanity as a whole – but never ever on behalf of those interests which actually did the colonising. As we have seen, even King Leopold felt obliged to present genocide as being in the better interests of the massacred – only nazi imperialism was entirely naked in asserting that it acted in the exclusive interests of the conqueror.

Britain and the USA are imperialist powers, both historically and presently. They are also, and within that limitation, democratic ones with powerful liberal and socialist political traditions (the socialist element much more articulated in the case of Britain), deep-rooted labour movements and generous scope for dissent. Those suffering from and opposing the depredations described in previous chapters have thus always been able to look to politicians, campaigners and broad public opinion in the metropolitan heartlands for support. Often they have not looked in vain. But often, too, their appeals have fallen on dusty ground. Imperialism has reached into the heart of the progressive wing of British politics down the years. The same story could be told regarding US or indeed French left-wing politics.

Today, the promotion of a "new imperialism" from the left is inevitably entwined with the question of neo-conservatism, which some have traced back to a left-wing point of origin. The connections between the two "neos" which dominated early 21st century global politics – neo-liberalism and neo-conservatism – are not straightforward. The present phase of imperialist policy was shaped by the neo-liberalism prevailing in the great powers from the early 1980s onwards – indeed, neo-liberalism created the imperative for a more aggressive imperialist policy, while the latter has in turn become a central method of expanding and sustaining the scope of neo-liberalism.

However, this does not mean that there is a complete identity of views between neo-liberals and neo-conservatives. US author Susan George has argued recently that "whereas all neo-cons are neo-liberals; all neo-liberals are not neo-cons." That does not seem to be right. They are not necessarily the same "party," It is true, as George suggests, that there are neo-liberals who would not necessarily have embraced neo-con imperialism. She identifies the founding father of what became neo-liberalism, Friedrich Hayek, as one. He certainly regarded his free-market fundamentalism as having universal application, but would most likely have deprecated the attempt to spread it by force and coercion, if for no other reason than because such an endeavour inevitably requires the build-up of the one thing he hated most of all – the state. That tradition continues to be represented by conservative libertarianism in US politics, and its 2008 presidential standard bearer Ron Paul. [3]

But what concerns us more here is those who advocate the reverse view – those who desire (or claim to desire) greater social equality in the USA and Britain, buttressed by state intervention in the economy, and therefore cannot be identified as neo-liberals, yet who also support the neo-conservative project for spreading the values of "the West" by force to other states. This might be a more internally consistent position if the governments doing the spreading were themselves of the left. Yet, as we know, the neo-conservative project was to all practical purposes driven by a US administration committed, *inter alia*, to tax cuts for the rich, the scrapping of workplace regulation, the disregard of the rights of labour, of the equality of women, and of the necessity of environmental protection – in short to the full neo-liberal agenda of the untrammelled exercise of corporate power. An administration which, moreover, attacked the civil liberties of the US citizen with a scope without real precedent. Only the neo-con "left" could then have been surprised when the self-same administration set out to govern conquered Iraq in exactly the same fashion.

It is not so much that they bought into the war aims of the Bush-Cheney administration but that they have wilfully ignored them, and supplied their own alternative aims instead, disconnected from the unfolding reality. Deception or self-deception, it was an operation mounted on a grand scale.

Of course, various objections can be raised against this line of argument – not least that the Blair government in Britain was in fact little different in its domestic priorities to those of the Bush administration. Indeed, it was a pioneer in the adoption of neo-liberal practice by a governing party of the centre-left. Nevertheless, Tony Blair felt obliged to pursue his pro-Bush policy with a heavy dose of liberal internationalist piety, and the pro-war trend in left-liberal academia and journalism also felt required to above all couch their arguments again and again in terms of a dispute within the left. He became the global spokesman for the neo-cons who affected to believe the social-democratic good life could and should be spread at the point of a George Bush bayonet.

Gladstonian Roots

And they have a back-story. Blair has acknowledged his debt to the man who may be regarded as the founding father of the idea of liberal imperialism – Prime Minister William Gladstone, the most commanding political figure of the Victorian era.

Gladstone's most sympathetic biographer Roy Jenkins acknowledges that "he had a sense...perhaps even a subconscious one of the superiority of white Anglo-Saxon men" which led him into a series of imperial adventures despite being elected on an anti-imperialist platform, acquitting more and more territory in the famous "fits of absent-mindedness". [4]

He led the British Empire, alternating with the Tory Benjamin Disraeli, at its pivotal period of transition, when modern imperialism emerged from the previous free-trade colonialism. The Marxist writer R. Palme Dutt made the same point as Jenkins more polemically: "The transition from the nineteenth-century liberal free-trade capitalism with its undercurrent of ceaseless colonial wars tactfully tucked away under a rose-coloured eiderdown of pacific sentiments, to the brazen aggressive and bellicose policies of modern imperialism found expression in the career of the Liberal party leader, Gladstone...No sooner had he taken office than he continued and carried forward to new heights [Tory] imperialist foreign policy, with ruthless coercion in Ireland and with violent military aggression for the conquest of Egypt and the Sudan." [5]

In fact, Gladstone differs from Blair in the show of reluctance he put up as he was impelled by events and interests allegedly beyond his control into one colonial adventure after another. He was forever, in the words of Victor Kiernan, "surreptitiously coming out upon his subject through a shrubbery of subordinate clauses, explaining to objectors why wealthy Britain could not afford to stop pushing opium on China." [6]

There was no such hand-wringing from his twenty-first century disciple although, if one wishes to be fair to Blair, it should be noted that he has not yet been caught in such an egregious act of corruption as Gladstone, who was a major investor in Egyptian bonds at the time he ordered military intervention in that country to secure its finances for the City. Blair instead signed up for the big bucks from the banks after laying down the burden of being a war leader – getting in just before the economic crash which his free-market fetishism had done a significant amount to produce.

Any residual element of reticence about foreign conquest was speedily abandoned in Gladstone's party. Lord Rosebery, his late-Victorian successor as Liberal leader, was more forthright: "It is on the British race...that rest the highest hopes of those...who seek to raise and better the patient masses of mankind." That the less patient masses of mankind were already in insurrection against the British race and, indeed, placed their highest hopes on its defeat, deterred his liberal lordship not one whit. [7]

The Labour Party started to succeed the Liberals as the principal expression of the progressive interest in British politics in the early years of the twentieth century, and had accomplished this operation within a generation. However, Labour's attachment to socialism was at first non-existent and later little more than nominal. Socialists were a part of the Labour coalition, but a very subordinate one. The new party's governing ideology was a mixture of trade unionism and liberalism. The liberal element was, in Labour hands, shorn of the Liberal Party's class commitment to the bourgeoisie whenever the latter's interests clashed with the trade unions, but not by any means of its equally potent ideological investment in a benevolent imperialism. That outlook was initially carried forward largely unmodified into the Labour Party by the more prosperous and skilled sections of organised labour, profiting from Britain's commanding position in the world economy. It was not, however, unchallenged, as we shall see. The two traditions within the British left on how to face the rest of the world were there from the beginning.

For and Against the Empire

If the pro-war left in Britain can therefore lean on a degree of precedent in its support for imperialism, so too can the anti-war movement in its opposition. Ernest Jones, one of the greatest leaders of the Chartist movement, wrote of the "Indian Mutiny" in 1857 that "there ought to be but one opinion throughout Europe on the Revolt of Hindustan. It is one of the most just, noble and necessary ever attempted in the history of the world." [8]

Jones was a revolutionary and generally speaking, the subsequent anti-imperialist tradition within the British left has been associated with the followers of Marx and of socialist revolution. The pro-imperialist trend in the working-class movement, on the other hand, was closely allied to the view that social change in Britain itself should be incremental, and guided by the educated, acting on behalf of the less enlightened. The acceptance of the inevitability, or even desirability, of the British Empire was most strongly advocated by Fabians and others who looked forward to only the most gradual displacement of capitalism within the metropolis. As Nicholas Owen puts it in the *Oxford University History of the Empire* "some Fabians saw imperialism as a necessity in an era of fiercely competing nation-states, to be pursued in the name of 'national efficiency' and turned, where possible, into progressive channels." [9]

The eminent Fabian George Bernard Shaw expressed the "internationalist" case for interference eloquently: "The notion that a nation has a right to do what it pleases with its own territory, without reference to the interests of the rest of the world, is no more tenable from the international socialist point of view…than the notion that a landlord has a right to do what he likes within his estate without reference to the interests of his neighbours." [10]

The contrary view was argued by the earliest socialist organisations. In 1885, for example, a Socialist League manifesto issued by William Morris and others concerning the British occupation of the Sudan argued: "A wicked and unjust war is now being waged by the ruling and propertied classes of this country, with all the resources of civilisation at their back, against an ill-armed and semi-barbarous people whose only crime is that they have risen against a foreign oppression which those classes themselves admit to have been infamous" – a war supported by "liberal imperialists" around Gladstone at the time, it should be added. [11]

By the time of the Boer War, popular support in Britain for imperialism was starting to come under strain. Sections of the Liberal Party were turning against a war which they saw as being fought for City interests. Nevertheless, a pro-Empire hysteria was still manufactured around the war's notable battles. A branch of the Social Democratic Federation in Scotland stood out against this by projecting "from the windows … a transparency of five feet, giving the statistics of deaths in war, deaths in concentration camps, the number of paupers, the number of unemployed in Britain, the famine deaths in India, and the famine deaths, emigration and evictions in Ireland" as a victory parade passed. [12]

And at the first conference of the British Socialist Party, held in 1912, Harry Quelch moved a resolution on "Socialism and Patriotism" explaining that "imperialism was the very opposite to patriotism. They were opposed to the Boer war, just as they were opposed to quite as iniquitous war many years before in Egypt, not because they had any special love for the administration of Mr Kruger, but because they believed that the Boers, or any other people, had a right to manage their own affairs in their own way." [13]

Labour Party founder Keir Hardie was broadly opposed to the Empire, asserting that "modern imperialism is in fact to socialists simply capitalism in its most predatory and militant phase." But not to all socialists. Ramsay MacDonald, Hardie's equal in eminence in the early Labour Party and later to become the first Labour Prime Minister, set out his stall in1901: "So far as the underlying spirit of imperialism is a frank acceptance of national duty exercised beyond the nation's political frontiers, so far as it is a claim that a righteous nation is by its nature restless to embark on crusades of righteousness wherever the world appeals for help, the spirit of Imperialism cannot be condemned...the compulsion to expand and assume world responsibility is worthy at its origins." By 1907, MacDonald was advocating a "socialist imperialism" based on Labour's "pride of race" which "to its subject-races...desires to occupy the position of friend." In an argument which anticipates Niall Ferguson's view that since there have always been empires, no-one could make a moral case against the British one, the Labour leader argued that the Empire was a "historical fact" which could no more be got rid of than the Stuart dynasty could be restored. [14]

This approach was not a great hindrance to Labour's electoral advance for the most part. Will Crook, the Labour Representation Committee candidate in the Woolwich by-election of 1903 was elected after announcing himself as a supporter of "robust imperialism". And there seems justice in the assessment of Chinese scholar Tingfu Tsiang, considering the view of the labour movement on imperialism in the early 1920s, that "the predominant characteristic of the reaction of British labour to British imperialism in Africa from 1880 to 1920 is acquiescence." Yet the attempt by Lord Meath, who we have already encountered, to make his Empire Day a focus for national imperialist fervour was resisted in 1813 by, among others, the London Society of Compositors, the Poplar Labour League, the Paddington and Kensington Labour Council and the National Union of Clerks. [15]

The high point of the influence of the anti-imperialist tradition was the TUC congress in 1925, before the great defeat of the 1926 General Strike, which declared "its complete opposition to imperialism" and resolved "to support the workers in all parts of the British Empire in organising trade unions and political parties in order to further their interests" and "to support the right of all peoples in the British Empire to self-determination, including the right to choose complete separation from the Empire." [16]

On balance, however, Labour Party leaders went a good deal further than Tsiang's "acquiescence." Phillip Snowden, subsequently to serve as a Labour Chancellor of the Exchequer, placed himself squarely in the Gladstonian tradition and argued in 1921 that China had no right to "deprive the rest of the world of access to her material resources" and "by no moral right may the ownership and control of the natural and material resources of a territory be regarded as the absolute monopoly of the people who happen to be settled there." [17]

That outlook, a variant on the Lockean philosophy regarding undeveloped property, informed the work of subsequent Labour governments to a considerable extent. Attlee's administration, while willing to bow to the inevitable and concede Indian independence, had no desire to liquidate the Empire. Its foreign secretary, Ernie Bevin, visualised the more intensive exploitation of its resources, while the renegade from Marxism John Strachey promoted ill-conceived ground-nut schemes for Africa. As Bayly and Harper put it: "Attlee and his generation were really nineteenth-century Whigs and their colonial policy was conceived in this vein. By no means convinced of the inherent value of territorial empire, they were none the less sure of the doctrine of the white man's burden." [18]

This attitude of course coloured Labour's view of the national liberation movements then developing apace across the Empire. In as neat a summation of the imperial left attitude as one could find, Rita Hinden, the highly influential secretary of the Fabian Colonial Bureau, said of a discussion in which Kwame Nkrumah, leader of the struggle for an independent Ghana, had put his case: "When Mr Nkrumah said 'we want absolute independence' it left me absolutely cool. Why?...British socialists are not so concerned with ideals like independence and self-government, but with the idea of social justice." [19]

Hinden's outburst rested on a highly-refined sense of the appropriate division of labour in the advancement of social justice across the world. Labour's policy on the colonies in 1956 made this clear: "Europeans, indeed, had brought with them modern knowledge and the machinery of Western civilisation. Moreover, they were experienced in public life and in political organisation. On the other hand, they could have done little without the cheap labour of the Africans, and material progress was speeded by the commercial enterprise of the Asians. All...were making their respective contribution." Political organisation from some, cheap labour from others. [20]

Loud echoes of Fabian-imperialist thinking have resurfaced in the course of the contemporary wars. Not for Blair and company the overt Labour racism which Hugh Dalton, one of the 1945 government's leading figures, candidly confided to his diary when turning down the offer of the post of Secretary of State for the Colonies in 1950: "I had a horrid vision of pullulating, poverty-stricken, diseased nigger communities...the more one tries to help them, are querulous and ungrateful..." The "ungrateful native" motif did resurface in some comments about Iraqis after the 2003 invasion, but generally not from the left wing of the pro-war coalition. However, the idea that national independence mattered little, and that social justice had to be imposed from without by those best placed to understand it, remained. [21]

Blair's approach to worldwide interventionism was best prefigured in the outlook of the senior official running the India Office in the 1920s, Sir Arthur Hirtzel. An imperialist, he said, holds that "the race to which he belongs is the noblest, and the civilisation and ideals for which it stands are the highest – are, in fact, so high, that all the world must needs accept them." [22]

Tony Blair devoted a large part of his energies as Prime Minister to that very task. He was not the first Labour Prime Minister to have represented imperialist interests, but more than any previous he presented this in terms of a messianic liberal/progressive internationalism, albeit one subordinated to a conservative US administration. As already noted and as the rest of the world hardly needs telling, British governments invading other countries was far from being a Blairite invention. Tory, Liberal, Labour, National and Coalition administrations have intervened around the world as a matter of course for the past two hundred years and more. It has rather been a novelty when, for want of a perceived need or, occasionally, of the necessary military or political wherewithal, they have refrained from doing so for a few years on the trot.

Blair's special contribution was to try to create a new range of justifications for this bad habit in the post-Cold War world, since neither "extending Christian civilisation" nor "halting the spread of Communism" any longer serve at the bar of public opinion.

Tony Blair's internationalism

Blair's first major address in this, his great work, was made in Chicago in 1999 while the war against Yugoslavia was raging. This speech became the foundation of his policy of violent intervention in other countries when he found it both desirable and possible. Ten years later, having laid down high office, he returned to Chicago to make a further speech, essentially saying that he still advocated his outlook of 1999.

Blair's supporters liked to present his first Chicago speech and his subsequent promotion of the Iraq War as an uninterrupted development of "internationalist interventionism." Of course, there are a number of political points of contact between the two wars, most notably in that the aggressors did not seek United Nations sanction in either case, in the sure and certain knowledge that it would have been refused.

But for the most part, Blair's arguments in support of the Balkans War did not fit even his own case for attacking Iraq, underlying the primarily expedient nature of such presentations. For example, he spent much of the 2002-2007 period asserting the need to intervene against "Islamic terrorism" above all. But the concept was entirely missing from the initial Chicago address, even though Bill Clinton was already blowing up aspirin factories in Sudan allegedly on account of it. This omission was of course rectified in the 2009 address.

In fact, Blair was mainly concerned in 1999 to justify interfering for other reasons, ethnic cleansing amongst them. He also argued that "one state should not feel it has the right to change the political system of another." Yet the desirability of regime change was to became one of his leading justifications for invading Iraq. [23]

In 1999, the Prime Minister outlined "five major considerations" which needed to be used when deciding whether or not to "intervene".

1. Are we sure of our case?
2. Have we exhausted all diplomatic options?
3. Are there military operations we can sensibly and prudently undertake?
4. Are we prepared for the long term?
5. Do we have national interests involved?

When applied to the Iraq War, Blair's difficulties in the realm of consistency immediately become apparent. Clearly this latter venture failed on points one and two, and did so at the time. Point three is obviously at best a shocking misjudgement when the history of the Iraq conflict is considered. Point five begs too many questions to be answered readily, but it should be noted that not only the anti-war movement but much of the establishment believed that the Iraq War did not meet any reasonable definition of "national interest." That then leaves just point four, which is not really a consideration on its own, but is entirely dependent on the other four being met before it can become operative. In any event the Anglo-US unpreparedness for anything other than military violence in Iraq has long been patent. And who is to judge if the criteria are met? The nebulous "international community," Blair said – which in the more concrete form of the UN Security Council was so adamantly opposed that it could not even be asked for a collective opinion in March 2003.

So a comparison of Blair's actual policy with his "Chicago doctrine" underlines the purely contingent nature of any justification advanced to justify an "internationalist-interventionist" foreign policy by its foremost spokesman worldwide. However, it is possible to identify two underpinning principles which unite the Labour premier's 1999 rhetoric and his 21st century actions.

The first was his determination to support the government of the USA, whatever the latter's outlook and intentions. In truth, there are very few "interventions" Britain could undertake without US involvement, whatever principles a Prime Minister may espouse. The Chicago speech was full of the same sycophantic and entirely uncritical praise of US policy under President Clinton that he later showered on Bush, securing a Medal of Freedom before the latter finally quit office. On other occasions, Blair described support for the US as "an article of faith" for him, for which a "blood price" would sometimes have to be paid. This was, of course, to prove to be far more than mere rhetoric.

The second Chicago principle was, appropriately enough in the city which lent its name to a whole "school" of free-market economic aggression, was a commitment to promote the interests of global neo-liberal capitalism – at the time its spectacular bust was still a decade away. "We are all internationalists now, whether we like it or not. We cannot refuse to participate in global markets if we want to prosper," Blair said in Chicago. And later: "We all understand the need to ensure flexible labour markets, to remove regulatory burdens and to untie the hands of business if we are going to succeed." That is an "internationalism" to which the chief executives of Exxon and Morgan Stanley could sign up to. Hands duly untied, they have since marched the world economy off a cliff.

And such was indeed the "internationalism" imposed by the occupation regime in Iraq, which left trade unions shackled by Saddam-era laws while a flat tax and privatisation were on the menu for big business. To call it internationalism at all, which invokes the traditions of solidarity with Republican Spain, of opposition to apartheid and support for movements against colonialism, is to rob the term of any meaning.

A better term is neo-colonialism. Even the "New Labour" government's less controversial foreign adventures bear its stamp. The dispatch of troops into diamond-rich Sierra Leone to prop up its regime against a rebel insurrection has generally been hailed as an unequivocal success for Blair's doctrine, for example. And, indeed, its negative consequences have been on a smaller scale than in Iraq, Afghanistan or the former Yugoslavia. But even in Sierra Leone, the reality has a familiar ring. Tom Porteous, an adviser to the Labour government on African policy at the time, writes that "…for all their faults, the rebels did represent the real grievances of many ordinary Sierra Leoneans against three generations of political leaders. Sierra Leone's political elite bore the greatest responsibility for creating the conditions for state failure and conflict. 'They stole our diamonds, they stole our gold' went the anthem of the rebel RUF, referring to the corruption of successive Sierra Leonean governments. And it was true." It was this elite which the British government's intervention restored to power, and eight years on from the intervention, Britain remains the de facto power in the country. [24]

Every worthy principle which might commend itself to an enlightened Western electorate has been pressed into service to support this rebranded neo-colonialism. But in the end the pretence that these are the actual reasons for war could not be sustained, even by the eloquence of Tony Blair. For example, feminism was invoked to justify the attack on Afghanistan. Afghan women were promised liberation by force from the misogyny of the Taliban. The following excerpt from an interview with Blair conducted by *Time* magazine speaks for itself:

Time: *Your wife chaired a press conference about the bad treatment of women in Afghanistan. What about Saudi Arabia? Do you approve of the way women are treated there?*

Blair: *I'm not going to get in the business of attacking the Saudi system.*

Time: *But you do attack the Afghan system.*

Blair: *Yes, but we're in conflict with the Taliban regime...At the present time I don't think it's very helpful to tell the Saudis how they should live.* [25]

So women's rights are dependent on their states' diplomatic positioning vis-à-vis Washington and London in the Blairite view of things. The consequences of this expedient view of rights became apparent in 2009 when the government Blair and company imposed on Afghanistan passed a law ordering Afghan women to submit to their husband's sexual urges on demand, and forbade them to leave their houses unescorted.

So the parameters of "humanitarian interventionism" are neatly identified in the little passage from the *Time* interview. They remain where Gladstone established them, as propaganda in the service of power. The Iraq War offered the most lurid proof of this, to the extent of shattering the pro-intervention coalition assembled around the first Gulf War and the attack on Yugoslavia.

Chapter Five
Dick Cheney's liberals

TWO PARALLEL wars have been fought in Iraq since 2003. One has been the illegal war of aggression initiated by George Bush and Tony Blair in alleged pursuit of non-existent weapons of mass destruction – a war actually designed to provide a base for US power throughout the region, underpin Israel's strategic position, and gain unfettered access to the country's resources. This war has cost up to a million lives, driven four million into internal or external exile, illegally incarcerated or tortured many more, incited sectarian strife, left the economy in ruins and destabilised the wider region.

And then there was the war fought by the progressive governments in the US and Britain to bring democracy and social justice to the people of Iraq. In that war, the invaders were to be greeted with flowers during a brief period of occupation before their armies handed over to a government representing the will of the Iraq people, taking only those illegal chemical and biological munitions away with them.

The alert reader will not have failed to notice that only one of these two wars actually happened. But what could previously have been described as "progressive opinion" worldwide, and in Britain and the US in particular, divided as to which was the one being fought. This stimulated a controversy along lines which would have been instantly familiar to William Morris and William Gladstone, from their opposed viewpoints.

In the Gladstone corner, behind the bellicose Prime Minister Blair, was a fairly shrivelled coterie of journalists and academics. Arguing from these media-friendly strongpoints ensured the pro-war and subsequent pro-occupation case a broad ventilation. However, the lack of any other support in those institutions and campaigns which traditionally constitute the left was a dramatic weakness.

Therefore when the "left" which backed Bush and Blair is examined, we do not need to look at trade union resolutions, nor at editorials in the main journals of progressive and socialist thought. It is the work of individuals who, in most cases, had spent the 1990s tip-toeing towards the imperial Fabian position. Their only effort to give themselves a more general political coherence – the appearance of the "Euston Manifesto" in 2006 – proved inconsequential and without any enduring impact. [1]

Journalists for war

On both sides of the Atlantic the "pro-war left" point of view has become most associated with Christopher Hitchens, memorably and accurately characterised by George Galloway as a "drink-soaked former Trotskyist popinjay." Hitchens, British by birth but long since based in the US, first caused a splash in Washington by spectacularly abandoning both friendships and principle in order to assist the anti-Clinton witch-hunt launched by the Republicans in Congress in the late 1990s. A former member of the International Socialists (now the SWP), Hitchens's writings over the last fifteen years or so seem designed to prove the truth of Eric Hobsbawm's aphorism that it is much easier to outrage the bourgeoisie than to overthrow it, taking "shock value" aim at Mother Teresa and God, while backing the masters of the universe on matters of substance, like war. To be fair, overthrowing the bourgeoisie has long since ceased to form part of his programme. His support for Bush did not come out of a clear sky. In relation to Iraq he was heavily influenced by the opinion of émigré Iraqi Kurds, neglecting the contrary views of Arab nationalism in the country (the latter representing of course the great majority of the population).

In Britain, a considerable number of left-ish journalists took up similar positions, including Nick Cohen of *The Observer*, David Aaronovitch, who migrated from the *Observer* to Rupert Murdoch's *Times* in the course of the war, John Lloyd of the *Financial Times*, and Johann Hari in *The Independent* – the last-named repented of his bellicosity as the Iraq cataclysm unfolded. A number of bloggers of variable distinction also put their shoulders to the interventionist wheel.

As this review of their forces indicates, such a line-up can scarcely be considered to constitute the "split" in the left that has sometimes been claimed for it. Compare the invade-Iraq party to that which rallied behind the

NATO attack on Yugoslavia in 1999. That really was a split – with any number of institutions, organs and leaders of the left on the pro-war side, from the Scottish TUC to *Tribune* newspaper left wing icons Michael Foot and Ken Livingstone. Over Iraq, however, the socialist, green, trade union, revolutionary and liberal lefts were actually more united than ever before. Moreover, this united left spoke for the great majority of the public at large, a somewhat novel circumstance for the left over the last thiry years.

However, the left-wing of the coalition to invade Iraq should be treated as more than a mere literary phenomenon, precisely because it did form a part of a much broader alliance, the key constituents of which were the US and British governments and their overtly neo-conservative and imperialist backers. As such, they supplied a line of defence and of explanatory justification for the war which its promoters in power came to sorely need. This was particulalry the case for Tony Blair's Labour Party, which constituted an ostensibly centre-left government. The party may have lost as many as half of its members in protest against the Iraq War. More than 140 of its backbench MPs voted against the aggression, and so would its party conference had an honest vote ever been held there on the subject. The existence of a "pro-war left" with broad media visibility was particularly useful to Blair under these circumstances, just as the British premier was useful to the US President in extending the range of political support for his agression.

This was, in summary, the left argument for backing Bush and Blair over the war:

Saddam Hussein was an especially evil dictator and his regime an abomination in the sight of all concerned for human dignity. The Iraqi people cried out to be freed from it. They had no means of achieving this liberation save through external invasion. Isolation and sanctions (which may not have been a good thing anyway) had failed. Of course, Bush and Blair may well have their own motives for attacking Iraq, but these, however suspect, weighed far less in the balance than the need to rid the world of Saddam and his regime. The more Blair, in particular, leant on moral arguments and the less on weapons of mass destruction and suchlike, the better. To oppose the war was to collude in Saddam remaining in power. The Iraqi people and their main organisations in exile were willing the invasion on. The left should stand with the oppressed, even if that would put them in some rum company.

In their own words, starting with David Aaronovitch: "I finally supported the war because I believed that Saddam Hussein was an almost uniquely dangerous and brutal dictator and that it was a stain on the Western nations that, before the 1990 invasion of Kuwait, we had so long encouraged or abetted him." For Christopher Hitchens the first reason for going to war was "the flouting by Saddam Hussein of every known law on genocide and human rights." [2]

The main weakness in this line of argument is obvious. It was not the reason the war was actually launched. The Pentagon's Paul Wolfowitz – a special favourite of Hitchens and Cohen – admitted that "the criminal treatment of the Iraqi people…is a reason to help the Iraqis but it's not a reason to put American kids lives at risk." Tony Blair, when gambling on the moral case for war amidst his losing PR battle in 2003, nevertheless acknowledged that this case was "not why we act."

Of course, the pro-war left did not confine itself to making its own special misjudgements over Iraq – it also retailed the same rubbish as everyone else in the war camp. They too pressed the "weapons of mass destruction" argument into play, hedging the bets they had placed on the "moral case" for war. David Aaronovitch, in one celebrated passage, went so far as to write: "I was never in favour of this war mainly because of the threats of terrorism or WMDs. Getting rid of Saddam (and therefore the myriad afflictions of the Iraqi people) was enough. But the weapons were the pretext on which the invasion was sold to a lot of people…these claims cannot be wished away in the light of a successful war. If nothing is eventually found, I – as a supporter of the war – will never believe another thing that I am told by our government, or that of the US ever again. And, more to the point, neither will anyone else…I repeat, those weapons had better be there." Murdoch's man has had to spend a fair amount of time wriggling around those last couple of sentences ever since. [3]

Hitchens, with his customary braggadocio, insisted that Saddam "certainly has nerve gas and chemical weapons" and even "that Saddam was partly a patron of al-Qaida". Both of those bold assertions were entirely untrue. [4]

Little remains to be written about these positions, so universally discredited have they become. The larger problem, however, was the issues not addressed in the pro-war left position, as identified when we considered Tony Blair's outlook – the human consequences of war, the implications for national sovereignty and the United Nations of the Bush-Blair policy, and the motives and intent of the US government in attacking Iraq.

These questions all formed a central part of the case against the invasion, yet the pro-war left brushed them aside in much the same manner as did their sponsoring governments. This was a double weakness in the case of those seeking to support the war from within the left, as they also form central pillars of the political outlook of most progressive opinion for the entire post-war period. Phrased slightly differently – a presumption against war and in favour of the peaceful resolution of disputes, the upholding of national sovereignty and international law, and opposition to US imperialism – these points were more or less common ground among movements and parties of the left for many years.

Take the most compelling first, the fact that any war brings the certainty of some loss of life and material destruction and the possibility of very considerable amounts of both. This is the most basic part of any case against war, of the presumption that every other avenue must be explored to the end first, that every leader should go the extra mile and then some to avoid embarking on a course which will send the innocent to early graves in large numbers. This prospect, above all, is the one that gets people out on the streets. Would anyone wish it otherwise? This, too, is what underlies the strict limitations laid down in international law on the sovereign right to wage war and the protocols of every attempt, however flawed, at international organisation. The left, even when not pacifist, has fought most strongly to uphold this principle for the last one hundred years both because it is the left's constituency, working people, which suffers disproportionately (sometimes almost exclusively) from war, but also because it holds out the vision of a better way to run the world.

Of course, this line of argument would be like pellets off a rhinoceros hide as far as a Dick Cheney would be concerned. It is more surprising that it registered so little on the pro-war left's radar. David Aaronovitch made one explicit stab, asking: "would 5,000 dead civilians be too many to justify war?" Not if chemical or biological weapons was found, or a link between those weapons and terrorist groups, he gave himself by way of an answer. None of the weapons were ever found, of course, but we do not know if he now regards the 160,000 dead civilians (on the most conservative of serious estimates, others range up to 1,000,000), or those absent weapons as too much or about right.[5]

No-one else on the pro-war left even grappled seriously with this dilemma. Aaronovitch himself obscurely observed that "we're not helped by the idea of war as last resort." Worse, Hitchens appeared to believe that war would actually be preferable to Saddam's peaceful departure from power. Before the war began he wrote that Secretary of State Colin Powell "can be faulted...for the welcome he gave to the idea of a safe haven for Saddam Hussein, thus greatly weakening the moral basis for the claim of regime change," although such a plan at that stage was the only way the Bush administration would abandon its invasion. [6]

As far as discarding of the importance of national sovereignty goes the pro-war left could correctly argue that this principle has never been an absolute one, to be held fast to in all times and all places. But, like the presumption in favour of peace, the presumption in favour of respecting the rights of states is a powerful one, because setting it aside can only be of advantage to the powerful. National sovereignty is, by and large, a weapon in the hand of the relatively weak of the world. It is a right which can be forfeited – if undertaking or threatening aggression against others, or in the event of genocide, as provided for by international law. Saddam Hussein might have been vulnerable on both counts at one time or another, but not in 2003, or for some years previously. Ignore the right to national sovereignty, except in such circumstances of prescribed extremity, and a green light is given to those with the power to ignore the rights of others to do so at will.

Sovereignty is deeply entwined with the idea, traditionally accepted without demur by most of the left, of self-determination. People have the right to shape their own future. And this is not just an abstract right. Self-determination, however arduous, leads to different outcomes, rooted in people's own experiences, struggles and cultures, than would be obtained through external determination or imposition, however allegedly "well-intentioned" the latter may be. That is one reason why self-determination increasingly became an accepted principle in international relations during the 1950s, 1960s and 1970s, when decolonisation was sweeping the Third World. It is also why, contrary to the illusions of Hitchens and co., most progressive Iraqi organisations – among the Arab population at least – did not support the Bush-Blair invasion of their country.

Closely related here is the question of disregarding agreed international law, mainly for these purposes embodied in the Charter of the United Nations. Can anyone from a liberal or left-wing tradition (not to mention many others) not have been embarrassed by then Foreign Secretary Jack Straw's squirming on this point, invoking Britain's right to ignore an "unreasonable veto" on the UN Security Council, when he knew full well that such a concept is legally non-existent.

Of those under review, only John Lloyd had a stab at this issue. In his pamphlet on Iraq and the "new world order" he wrote that "the international scene is too dynamic and troubled for a reassertion of national sovereignty, or of unilateralism on the part of any state, or of a multilateralism which achieves only stasis." He argued that sovereignty has been eroded by economic interdependence and various atrocities and does not, in any event, apply to "failed states."

It is by now obvious that the "dynamism" Lloyd saw in the "international scene" has been a good deal more deleterious to the right of sovereignty than it has been to "unilateralism on the part of any state," since such unilateralism was the governing principle of Bush and Cheney's Washington. That underlines the central argument against ignoring the right to national sovereignty – only powerful unilateralists can get away with it. The only new world order which could arise on such a basis would be founded on the acquiescence of everyone else, with varying degrees of abasement, in the unchallengeable authority of the great unilateral superpower. That "unilateral moment" is now starting to pass in any case, in part because of the rejection of Lloyd's view of the world by most of the US people themselves. [7]

Elsewhere, in a farewell article in the *New Statesman*, having quit because the editor had permitted another contributor to call him a "reactionary," Lloyd also suggested that the only alternative to war was "aggressive containment of Iraq", which would have caused suffering for the population, and was in any case lacking United Nations support. [8]

The incongruity of the implication that war would cause less suffering to the civilians (clearly not the case, as Iraqi experience has since established), or that the lack of UN support for sanctions could bestow on Britain and the USA the authority to start a war without the merest vestige of UN endorsement is apparent. Lloyd's logic was that the will of the United Nations is only worth consideration if it coincides with that of Washington. He also firmly nailed his colours to the mast on the sovereignty issue, arguing that tyrants should be stripped of their inviolability. This begs several questions. Who dubs a tyrant a tyrant and who shall decide which tyrants should be stripped of their power, and when? Could Russia, say, decide to ignore the sovereignty of the House of Saud? Or India that of the government of Pakistan? Clearly this would turn international relations into a jungle, a difficulty Lloyd has resolved by enlisting himself in the service of the biggest tiger.

The third area of neglect was an examination of the motives of the United States government. Motivation matters. Hitler had a case against the Versailles Treaty's treatment of Germany, for example, which was widely acknowledged on both the right and the left in the 1920s. But an examination of Hitler's own internal and international programme should have led (and indeed did, for most) to greater weight being given to considerations other than the injustice done to Germany in 1919 in the debates over how to respond to his regime.

Lloyd alluded to the matter of the nature of US power in the New Statesman article mentioned above, only to dismiss the concern. "US imperialism, in the view of a now resurgent part of the left, is composed of a mixture of things: efforts to control energy resources, principally oil; the repression of the Palestinians in order to ensure the future security of the US 'client state' Israel; a US refusal to tolerate any power in the world that counter balances its own; a hatred of all cultures other than its own, and a determination to dilute and destroy such cultures to make the world passively receptive to American values and merchandise."

Curiously, he supplied no commentary on his list of attributes of US imperialist positions. In fact all except the suggestion that the US officially "hates" other cultures were either publicly declared US policy under Bush or a reasonable description of it. Perhaps Lloyd regarded antipathy to US policy as self-evidently nonsensical.

By simply ignoring the three cardinal points of principle outlined above, the "cruise missile liberals" denied the left any coherent basis for forming an analysis of world politics, any prescription for a better world order or, in the end, any position other than hitching itself to the tailfins of the US presidency and hoping that the latter will act for the best more often than not.

Lloyd did sketch the "bare bones" of a future world order. Its four points were "orderly and peaceful relations between states"; increased effort to alleviate poverty and disease; to "protect on the part of governments, the security of all citizens" and where this provision is flouted for the expediency of external intervention be considered *at the United Nations*; and finally, for the "major states of the world" to reach an agreement on the basis for a global system of security.[9]

It is obvious that even if this thin list of proposals had been adopted by the world's rulers the attack on Iraq would not have passed muster. The invasion directly negated point one and flouted the provisions of point three. Even point four would have had to have been set aside, since most of the "major states" however defined (including Russia, China, India, France and Germany) opposed the invasion. Lloyd did not appear sensitive to this inconsistency.

So, was Saddam so wicked that considerations of international law, US imperial motivation and the desirability of avoiding unnecessary death and destruction should all have been set aside? And, even if he were indeed as wicked as that, was war the only way to do something about it? Nearly all the progressive Iraqi opposition to Saddam answered negatively to both questions.

Here Christopher Hitchens was deeply revealing, both as to his preference for war in despite of alternatives, and as to his own view the place of the US government in world affairs. He wrote, in November 2002:

"Saddam Hussein is not going to survive. His regime is on the verge of implosion. It has long passed the point of diminishing returns…it is a pyramid balanced on its apex and when it falls all the consequences of a post-Saddam Iraq will be with us anyway....the choices are two and only two – to experience these consequences with an American or international presence or watch them unfold as if they were none of our business. (I respect those who say that the United States should simply withdraw from the Middle East, but I don't respect them for anything but their honesty.)" [10]

Hitchens was even witless enough to describe this as the "clinching point" in the case for war. In fact, it was the opposite. If Saddam was certain to fall *with or without war*, then the argument for invasion disappeared on the instant. At most attack would only hurry along the inevitable fall of the inverted pyramid. But, as noted earlier, avoiding war was not the concern of Christopher Hitchens. The only way to read this passage is that he desired war in order to solidify the "American presence" in the Middle East, to ensure that the post-Saddam Iraq was built up under US tutelage, rather than as the free endeavour of a self-liberated Iraqi people.

Parenthetically, it should be added that Hitchens had changed his geopolitical perspective by January 2003, writing that "only the force of American arms, or the extremely credible threat of that force, can bring a fresh face to power" in Iraq. Perhaps the implications of his position had broken on him sufficiently to realise that a rapid reappraisal was required if he was to be of continued service to the Pentagon. [11]

Anyway, Hitchens has had his wish. Iraq struggles to emerge into its future with the elephant of foreign occupation on its back. It is "experiencing the consequences" of an "American presence" in spades. Perhaps this has been a surprise to him. Writing before the invasion, he claimed on the basis of who knows what information that "a strong presumption has been established against any uniformed tutelage", and that the US military role post-invasion would be restricted to the delivery of supplies. Some supply-delivery operation that turned out to be. [12]

The experience of contemporary imperialist occupations pre-Iraq ought to have been a warning that the situation would not work out so rosily. However, Hitchens believes that all these occupations were good things. He airily dismisses the notion that the occupations of much of the former Yugoslavia and Afghanistan could even merit the mild epithet "quagmire". It is hard to improve on the word as a description of Karzai's Afghanistan, where the government's writ does not run outside the capital, ministers are regularly murdered while there is no law but the warlord and the only hope is dope; or of Bosnia with its intransigently unreconciled communities; or of occupied Kosovo, where ethnic cleansing of Serbs has proceeded to a far more complete conclusion than the erstwhile campaign of the Serbs against Kosovans, under the eyes of a UN force mainly notorious for boosting up the local sex trade. [13]

For Hitchens, the early days of the Iraq occupation were a moment for hubris. On April 9 2003, he rejoiced "'Stop the War' was the call. And the war is indeed stopping," adding that arms inspectors were indeed to be given more time. A little later he crowed: "Look back if you care to and read the wild alarmist predictions that were made. There would be a military quagmire. The Arab street would arise, led by fans of Osama bin Laden, and wreak revenge. Israel would seize the chance to cleanse the West Bank and Gaza of the Palestinians. Turkey would invade northern Iraq. Weapons of chemical and neurological horror – the very ones that Saddam did not possess – would be hurled indiscriminately. Heaps of civilian corpses would rise." [14]

In fact, almost all these predictions have come true. There has been a military quagmire, even by the exacting Hitchens definition of a quagmire. The "fans of bin Laden" have indeed wrought hideous revenge in Iraq. Turkey has launched armed incursions into northern Iraq and asserts the right to keep on doing so. Israel has used the opportunity to ditch even the flimsy "road map" to peace and proceed with the bantuisation of Palestine and, in January 2009, a murderous assault on Gaza. There are indeed heaps of civilian corpses in Iraq, if the 160,000 acknowledged by the Iraqi government (or the 1,000,000 plus claimed by *The Lancet*) qualifies as a Hitchens heap. And as for the "weapons of horror" – the anti-war movement actually predicted that they were most likely not there at all, as indeed they were not. Hitchens's opponents were, in point of fact, correct on issue he himself chose to berate them with. Nothing daunted, Hitchens became a voluble supporter of the occupation, enthusiastically welcoming the US destruction of the resistance-controlled city of Fallujah at the end of 2004, regretting only that "the death toll is not nearly high enough." [15]

Lloyd too was full of hope in 2003: "Many therefore see it as incumbent on the states which do make the intervention...to establish a rule in Iraq which is both efficient and just, and to then follow through with a renewed effort to bring agreement between Israelis and Palestinians in order to realise the potential of a transformative (sic) moment." Likewise Aaronovitch: "...there have been very few suicide attacks, not the thousands confidently anticipated by George Galloway...hundreds of thousands have not died (or even scores of thousands, or even one score). There has not been a massive humanitarian crisis." Commentary on these pious aspirations of the liberal conquering class, aspirations being falsified even as they wrote them, is now almost redundant. The only "transformative moment" coming up was the clear display of the limitations of US military might in subduing a resisting people. [16]

Here, one last time, is Christopher Hitchens: "some countries inflict torture or murder at random, since the pedagogic effect on the population is even greater if there is no known way of avoiding the terror. Caprice, also, lends an element of relish to what might otherwise be the boring and routine task of repression. However, most governments will have the grace (or the face) to deny that they do this. And relatively few states will take photographs or videos of the gang rape and torture of a young woman in a cellar and then deposit the evidence on the family's doorstep."

That is as good a description as any of the barbaric goings-on at Abu Ghraib. Hitchens proclaimed himself shocked by the latter when the hideous photographs of the tormenting of prisoners (themselves illegally detained without procedure) saw the light of day. Well he might – he was just applying for citizenship of one of those "few states" which did indeed take such photographs.

He had, however, little right to be indignant and none to be surprised. The torture photographs from the prison in the desert are the pornography of imperialism, familiar to all with eyes to see for the last 200 years. Imperialism, to paraphrase, means Abu Ghraib wherever and whenever it is practised. [17]

Oliver Kamm

Hitchens was a pro-war agitator writing for immediate effect in support of a cause urgently needing advocacy. Others tried to develop the more substantive arguments in favour of neo-conservatism over a broader historical canvass. So here we shall introduce Oliver Kamm. Once a hedge fund manager and energetic pro-war blogger, now a leader writer on *The Times*, Kamm could be said to touch base with almost every calamity world capitalism has visited on the planet this century. Nevertheless, his *Anti-Totalitarianism: The left-wing case for a neo-conservative foreign policy* developed the argument for imperialist intervention in a fashion which explicitly brought out the continuity of the pro-Iraq War left with the pro-NATO left of previous historical phases of support for US aggression around the world.

Kamm was not typical of the pro-war left. His claim to be on the left at all was rather thin. He left the Labour Party in the early 1980s and actually voted Conservative at the 2005 general election, since the Labour candidate in his constituency was insufficiently Blairite.

His politics are those of an unmodified Cold War warrior, hostile not merely to communism but even to those social democrats, like Willy Brandt, who sought détente with it. He has collaborated with others – more Tories than Labour – in setting up the Henry Jackson Society, named after the late US senator, to promote the case for "intervention" in support of democracy around the world by Western powers.

His book addressed not only the arguments around the Iraq War – "the most far-sighted and noble act of British foreign policy since the founding of NATO" – but other episodes in the history of what he regards as the left's vacillating opposition to totalitarianism. [18]

Three political positions informed both Kamm's treatment of history – unconditional anti-Sovietism; an equally robust pro-Atlanticism and an unyielding refusal to allow the category of "imperialism" to enter into his treatment of international politics.

He cleaved to the same simple view of twentieth century world politics as the self-described "very right-wing" historian Andrew Roberts. It was a series of confrontations between liberal democracy, mainly represented by Britain and the USA, and a succession of varieties of "totalitarianism" – nazism, communism and today political Islam.

"Totalitarianism" is itself a post-war invention. In the 1930s it was commonplace to speak of "the dictators", lumping together Hitler, Mussolini and Stalin. That term would not do for Anglo-American propaganda after the war, since so many of the world's dictators were by then Washington's boon companions.

"Totalitarianism", which by that time meant communism alone, was invented as a basis for the necessary discrimination. US academic-turned-diplomat Jeanne Kirkpatrick, a pioneer neo-conservative cited by Kamm, used it to develop a theory to justify positive ties with right-wing and even fascist regimes while maintaining unyielding hostility to the socialist states.

On this theory, one could get cosy with Indonesia's Suharto or Chile's Pinochet, responsible for the slaughter of thousands (hundreds of thousands in the case of the former) while remaining intransigent towards, say, Kadar's Hungary, which killed next to nobody, on the grounds that the latter regimes were incapable of peaceful reform.

Even in Kirkpatrick's own terms, this position has been amply confounded by events, an early example of neo-conservatives misjudging the world. However, what is worse about this reading of history is what is left out in its liberal democracy-versus-a-procession-of-bad-guys schema. Imperialism is the missing factor, unarguably one of the defining elements in twentieth century world politics and at the very centre of those of the twenty-first to date. In fact, Kamm twice referred to imperialism in his book. On both occasions the qualifying adjective is "Soviet". In considering the politics of the 1930s, he describes the Soviet Union as "an imperialist power…brutal in its foreign conduct." [19]

Setting to one side the lack of any evidence to sustain such a description of Soviet policy in the 1930s, it requires a mighty myopia to not so much as mention the fact that at the period under review the British Empire held a quarter of the Earth's surface and more than a fifth of its population in varying degrees of coercion and that this circumstance shaped the politics of the left both in Britain itself and elsewhere.

The important truth that Britain before the war, like the USA after it, was (and is) a liberal democracy is inadequate on its own for considering its place in world politics. Indeed, it would not be taken seriously anywhere outside the most closed circles of the Anglo-Saxon political-media-academic world.

Both before and after World War Two Britain and the USA were also aggressive powers holding down peoples and nations in almost every corner of the world for the profit of their ruling interests. To this end, they directly oppressed and killed very large numbers of people and they have also maintained a variety of dictatorial regimes, some of which are still with us, in the Middle East above all, as outlined in chapter three.

This point Kamm mildly acknowledged – US policy was "compromised by tactical alliances with authoritarian regimes" – but attributed to the exigencies of the Cold War. His view is that by adopting a foreign policy which includes overthrowing by force all manner of unpleasant governments, the neo-conservatism of today can atone for the perhaps-unavoidable sins of yesterday's pre-neo conservatism.

He did not give any consideration as to other arguments advanced on the left to explain Bush's foreign policy. Because the USA is a "liberal democracy," apparently the motivation for its international conduct does not require inspection. Thus, his book did not address the obvious issue of control of the oil resources of the Middle East, nor the uncritical support which most US politicians give to Israeli expansionism. He played down the work of the Project for a New American Century and the other evidence that the Bush administration was bent on an aggressive assertion of US hegemony in the world well before the al-Qaida attacks on New York and Washington.

Kamm gets in the muddle usual among supporters of the Bush-Blair post 9/11 policy when discussing the motivation for those attacks. He writes: "...the terrorists of 9/11 were not making a statement about poverty and oppression. Rather, they were acting out an ideological imperative of striking at the institutions of Western civilisation: constitutional government, international commerce and a civilian-controlled military." [20]

Like Tony Blair Kamm found it more convenient to simply ignore the possibility of any secular basis for the actions of terrorists, since that would require an examination of Anglo-US policy. Politically, it is easier by far for the war party to treat "terrorism" as the product of a fanaticism and medievalism which can only be extirpated by violence.

Again, the serious neo-conservatives fall down in taking the motivations of Bush and Blair at exactly their own righteous valuation, while characterising the political objectives of those opposing them with crude and cartoon-like phrases – "totalitarian" or "fanatical," or "appeasers" of the totalitarian fanatics. When considering the rulers of the "liberal democracies," their laudable values mean the nobility of their motives can be taken for granted, even when they have led to an astonishing number of deaths and vast suffering. But for their opponents, their demands and motivation can be ignored in favour of a strict focus on their tactics – "terrorism".

"They have declared war on us," Kamm asserted in relation to the Islamic terrorists. So "we" must respond. The argument as to whether 9/11 was an act of war or a crime has been well-rehearsed. Had it occurred almost anywhere in the world other than the USA it would, perforce, have been considered a crime and addressed by all available national and international legal mechanisms. That is what happened, for example, after Pakistani-based militants had laid waste to the centre of Mumbai in an assault in 2008. The world, including the US itself, urged caution on the Indian government. Only the USA, more or less, is in a position to treat such an outrage as an act of war and permitted to proceed on that basis.

But even if one does consider 9/11 an act of war, only the most Anglo-Saxon-centric commentator could consider it the *start* of the war. As described in Chapter Three, for millions the "war" began more than one hundred years ago with the incremental imperialist intrusion into the Ottoman Empire and has been sustained with barely a blink ever since. Democratic regimes, plundered resources and millions of foreshortened lives lie in its wake – all of them in the Middle East, north Africa and south Asia.

Kamm would have the "war" declared on the USA as coming out of a cloudless sky. To allow the real history outlined in the present volume to be as much as entered in the record would be to countenance the contemporary sin of "root causism" or, as it might have been put in more enlightened times, to endeavour to understand why what is happening is happening, rather than being content with Bush's bible-and-bomb response.

In fact, looking for the roots of disagreeable developments has a very long and honourable pedigree. For an example of ruling class root-causism, the Victorian Prime Minister Lord Salisbury, whose record of foreign interventionism would make even Dick Cheney blanch, insisted on not merely condemning the Phoenix Park murder of Britain's overlord in Dublin by Irish nationalists but also on drawing out the "close connection between the crimes and the [British] government policy which has caused it." [21]

"Root causism" is actually the only attitude compatible, not just with rational debate, but with any hope of securing a solution to the problem of "terrorism," Most violence so described derives from social reality and serious forces – oppressed classes, nations or peoples – sustain it. Under those circumstances, even if you regard the demands which terrorists fight for as undesirable and the deliberate killing of civilians as unacceptable, a political response alongside, or for preference instead of, a military one is essential.

In fact, the great majority of conflict in the world today – and for years past – has been born as the child of imperialism, either in the latter's direct actions or as a consequence of the global and regional "orders" it has imposed. Since the category of imperialism goes unrecognised by Kamm and the rest of the left-wing neo-conservatives they spare themselves the labour of fashioning any alternative political response.

Instead, a mere call to arms to people the barricades of "liberal democracy" under unjust assault from the barbarians without is sufficient. This is a comforting bromide for the complacent inhabitants of traditional *Daily Express* Britain, who have never been able to bear the idea that what happens to "us over here" is a consequence of what "we " have done "over there."

But it is of no use in shaping a left-wing foreign policy. A consistent anti-imperialism, challenging the vast economic inequalities and abuses of political power underpinned by the military power of the USA above all, which are beholden to the narrowest of class interests in the metropolitan countries, should be at the centre of the left's view of the world – a world in which foreign and domestic policy cannot conceivably be disentangled.

Others on the left may take a different approach and base their perspective on international law and the United Nations. Kamm was uncharacteristically diffident in his handling of international law, the upholding of which has been an idea nearly universally supported on the British left for most of the post-war period. "I am not competent to discuss the legality of the Iraq War," he averred, before going on to sympathise with the opposition of the US administration to a "rules-based system that stands outside and above politics." [22]

Transferred to a national scale, such a view would mean the end of the rule of law. On the international plane, it merely removes one of the shackles that the many less powerful countries of the world may put on the behaviour of the more powerful, since in practice only the latter are in a position to take advantage of a regime of international lawlessness.

Kamm squared this circle to his own satisfaction by asserting that "the international order, unlike a constitutional democracy, is anarchic." Even if that were true, acquiescing in such an anarchy has never been a "left-wing" approach to the world. And if it is true, and might alone is right, then all one can safely predict is that terrorism will become more popular as the weapon of choice of the less than mighty. [23]

Furthermore, once the precedent is established and international law relegated to the second division of considerations, how can we be sure that those who are able to invade other countries with relative impunity – mainly the USA – will stick with such apparently agreeable targets as Saddam's Iraq? Does Kamm have his own target list for invasion?

To ask the question reveals that the neo-con "left" has no positive programme of "intervention" of their own. Their function is only to put the best possible face on a targeting strategy drawn up by the likes of Bush and Cheney in their own interests and to advance their own economic and political agenda. In fact, this was a "left-wing foreign policy" which was sub-contracted to some of the most right-wing politicians on the planet for the entirety of its execution.

Attacking the Peace Party

The "pro-war left" was most upset to find itself in such a small and increasingly reviled minority among their former comrades so it is unsurprising that they devoted a lot of their energy not only to making the case for war but also to denouncing the anti-war movement.

Nick Cohen did particular service on this front, using his bully pulpit in two normally left/liberal organs, *The Observer* and the *New Statesman*, to continually denounce the peace party. "The interests of opposing George Bush or Tony Blair or the oil corporations were put ahead of the interests of an oppressed people...to oppose the war was to agree that the Iraqis should continue to live in a prison state," he asserted. Likewise, when two million British people marched against the planned invasion of Iraq in 2003, Christopher Hitchens fulminated that "...there are not enough words in any idiom to describe the shame and disgrace of this," since it would have meant leaving Saddam in control of most of Iraq. [24]

The suggestion that unless one is prepared to advocate armed invasion of a country one shares moral responsibility for the actions of its government constitutes a novel absurdity. The idea that the anti-war movement, by opposing the invasion of Iraq was thereby complicit in the atrocities of the Saddam regime rested on the notion that one must approve of a regime if one fails to call for a foreign invasion to overthrow it. On such logic, Hitchens, Cohen *et al* would approve of the Saudi regime, the Burmese junta and so on since they have yet to demand that these despotisms be destroyed by externally-applied force majeure. The truth is that they have sub contracted that part of their critical faculties to the US administration, which alone decides which brutal regimes it suffers to survive (or even to sustain) and which must be overturned.

Following the same reasoning it would be fair to insist that the liberal imperialists bear a moral responsibility for the atrocities of the invaders who they cheered on every step of the way. Their spirit haunts the photographs from Abu Ghraib. Is that a Christopher Hitchens dropping the hood over the head of the prisoner, John Lloyd holding the leash on the slavering Alsatian, Nick Cohen kneeling over the corpse giving a cheerful thumbs-up? So it would seem.

The venom of Cohen's sallies against George Galloway, the Muslim Association of Britain and the Stop the War Coalition, not sparing the present author from *ad hominem* assault, went some way to concealing the embarrassing fact that he was initially himself opposed to the "war on terror." [25]

This is what he wrote in October 2001: "So there you have it. A Prime

Minister who discards parliamentary democracy and cabinet government, then spins against his colleagues so that his indiscriminate love for the United States can override national interests. Britain reduced to being the American poodle my comrades on the left always said it was. Perhaps it is time to embrace the Pinters and Pilgers as brothers and accept that, although they got Kosovo horribly wrong, they have Afghanistan just right." [26]

This cogent analysis did not long endure. Perhaps noting that Hitchens's megaphone apostasy was prospering on the other side of the Atlantic, Cohen rapidly became a convert to the cause of the Pentagon-sponsored Iraqi National Congress led by Ahmed Chalabi. He seemed confused as to its nature, at one point referring to its "guerrillas" which would apparently carry on fighting if Saddam was replaced by another dictator after the war. The INC had no guerrillas, and conducted struggle strictly in the restaurants of Georgetown. In a startling piece of journalistic misjudgement, Cohen decided to build up this made-in-Washington front by comparing Saddam unfavourably to apartheid South Africa, of all places.

"Unlike the African National Congress, however, the Iraqi National Congress hasn't become the toast of left-liberals. Its claim for committed support is at least as good because, in fairness to mass-murdering white supremacists, the old South Africa drew the line at dropping chemical weapons on neighbouring states and rioting Soweto school children. Nearly all South African whites – 16 per cent of the population – enjoyed wealth and partial freedom under apartheid." [27]

The INC-ANC parallel might collapse at the point where one places Nelson Mandela, who endured 28 years incarceration for his cause with dignity and resilience, next to INC leader Ahmad Chalabi, a long-exiled spiv with a conviction for bank fraud in Jordan and a wallet stuffed with the Pentagon's lucre. It also requires overlooking that Mandela secured overwhelming popular support in South Africa's post-apartheid elections, while Chalabi secured no seats at all in Iraq's elections in 2006. The INC only remained a player in Iraq's politics as long as it secured a massive monthly subvention from the US armed forces for providing them with intelligence against anti-occupation Iraqis, before Washington tired of Chalabi's Iranian connections.

Or does the parallel disintegrate when one considers the "good-neighbourliness" of the apartheid regime, which illegally occupied Namibia for years (one must acknowledge that opposing illegal occupations not *per se* a problem for Cohen), invaded Angola at Washington's behest and funded the Renamo guerrilla movement in Mozambique as it slaughtered countless thousand of civilians in an effort to destabilise a regime doing its utmost to build a decent life for its people.

And, no, the apartheid regime did not drop chemical weapons on "rioting Soweto schoolchildren". They shot them dead year after year (or flung them out of the upper floors of police stations by way of variety). Is this morally superior to administering death from chemical poisoning? And those who cannot distinguish between a demonstration for freedom and a "riot" (the term used by the apartheid authorities in their time and by Cohen in ours) should perhaps not be given much more attention.

But this odious comparison, which Cohen himself selected to make his point, does lead back to the now familiar question: Did Cohen advocate US or British military action to invade South Africa and overthrow the South African government during the apartheid years? Or did he advocate economic and diplomatic sanctions, allied to support for the ANC? The answer is plain.

Of course, the ANC never asked for an Anglo-US invasion of South Africa to end apartheid. Unlike Chalabi, it stood on its own feet without neo-conservative sponsorship, and its guerrilla fighters were not figments of a long-liquid-lunch imagination. The extent of the Pentagon's campaign to suborn journalists in Britain and the USA into promoting Chalabi as the man to "save Iraq" has since been widely exposed. Judy Miller of the *New York Times* was disgraced for her credulous retailing of Chalabi's Cheney-sponsored spin. Cohen has got off lightly, by contrast.[28]

But rather than acknowledging that he had been the victim of a "sting," Cohen simply dismissed the misinformation he had sedulously retailed as being of no significance. In a vituperative attack on Robin Cook in *The Observer*, the columnist's response to the fact, then rapidly becoming apparent, that the weapons of mass destruction which were offered as the reason for war were non-existent, was "so what?"[29]

So this, apparently Cohen found it unexceptionable for the government to lie to Parliament and the public about going to war. But he did do irony. At the very moment when, it has now been revealed, British soldiers were brutalising to death Iraqi civilians in the south of their country, he described the army as "…the armed wing of Amnesty International." [30]

While the army was doing Amnesty's work, the vast anti-war movement was moving him to a frenzy of abuse. He wrote of the mass demonstrations in 2003 that "the masses can't work out why they're not being addressed by someone they've seen on the telly," dismissing those who protested for peace as "Pinters, Trotskyists, bishops, actresses and chorus girls" and later, simply as "gormless." [31]

If Cohen redeemed himself, it was only by being generous enough to write his own obituary as a political commentator. He wrote in his 2006 book *What's Left?*: "Rather than accept the psychological consequences of confessing error, people lose their bearings. They talk only to friends. They imagine conspiracies as they seek the worst possible motives for their critics. They retreat into coteries and speak in code." [32]

The passage was ostensibly about the hapless John Major and his Tory government of the 1990s. But nobody was fooled – like those painters who love to drop their own likeness into the back of a crowd scene, Cohen decided to insert himself into the middle of his book and see if anyone noticed. After all, it fits. His error in using his platforms in the liberal press to cheerlead for the Iraq War was a colossal one. Many writers and some politicians who took the same pro-war position in 2003 have admitted their mistake and tried to move on. Cohen instead mounted a sustained and abusive campaign against those who were – there is no way of gilding the lily – right on the most important issue of world politics this century when he was wrong.

He has since "talked only to friends." They include Paul Wolfowitz, the one-time Pentagon architect of the war, who took Cohen out to dinner. Presumably that was payback for Cohen's 2002 touting of Chalabi. He has also retreated into the coterie of Britain's residual neocon circles. And he has of course imputed the worst of possible motives to those who disagreed with him, as we have seen. And instead of a restoring confession of error he wrote *What's Left?*, which was based on the assumption that the rest of the left got everything wrong. Were ever bearings so completely lost?

Cohen's central charge against the anti-war movement was that it compromised its principles by demonstrating alongside people who are not liberals or socialists. This was buttressed by the creation of a spurious "Islamofascism," which no one has yet defined satisfactorily, and no conceivable definition of which fits the many Muslims who campaigned alongside the Stop the War Coalition. Its promiscuous use by the pro-war party amounted to little more than an attempt at political intimidation directed against a minority already facing deep-rooted racism in British society.

Indeed, as the debate about the Iraq conflict itself moved towards a more or less consensus of opposition, the pro-war liberals moved on to a second front by way of displacement activity – denouncing "political Islam" in terms often indistinguishable from Muslim-baiting, particularly aimed at those Muslims who played a leading part in the anti-war movement. The latter's views on women's rights or sexuality were often misrepresented in the most cartoonish way by Cohen and others. It is all of a piece with the sustained wave of Islamophobic provocation by British politicians and media in recent years, with the Muslim community being required to jump through more and more hoops to establish their right to be included in political discourse

In any case, it was by and large better to march for peace with people who are not liberals than it was to support a war headed by a not-in-the-least-bit liberal George Bush. But in Cohen's demonology, the baddies are all of the one faith. Anyone who was proud to march with hundreds of thousands of British Muslims in 2003 was fooled by a bunch of theocratic fanatics. Once upon a time, the left would have been united in regarding such an outlook as indistinguishable from racism.

Nor was Cohen's polemical method in *What's Left?* in the least bit original. In one passage he suggested that since the Stop the War Coalition organised demonstrations with the Muslim Association of Britain, and the Muslim Association of Britain was associated with the Muslim Brotherhood, and the Muslim Brotherhood looked up to Yusuf al-Qaradawi, and Qaradawi has made undoubtedly offensive remarks about gays and women ... then the Stop the War Coalition is sexist and homophobic. Even Senator McCarthy might have expired through exhaustion before arriving at Cohen's destination.

It would be an easy game to play. Nick Cohen writes for the *Evening Standard*, which is published by Associated Newspapers, which owns the

Daily Mail, which is not just homophobic but Tory so Nick Cohen is ... Conservative? He was getting there, as shown by his subsequent preference for Boris Johnson over Ken Livingstone as London's Mayor, and by signing up as a columnist for the explicity Tory *Standpoint* magazine. Again, he was following one pace behind Christopher Hitchens, who backed Goerge Bush's re-election in 2004. When a star-struck Johann Hari interviewed Hitchens for the *Independent* in 2004, he was mortified that his hero failed to rule out "settling down on the American right," only excluding the nativist "Buchanan-Reagan right" as his political home. Hari's description of Hitchens as "slump[ing] into neoconservatism" seems to have provided Cohen with a sort of personal road map. [33]

Alliances between people of otherwise differing views are in fact the stuff of any serious mass campaign. People come together for a specific objective without signing up to everything that the other may believe in. That presents no difficulties as long as everyone leaves their other opinions at the door and does not seek to use the movement as a platform to grind their particular axes. It turns out that this was the approach taken by Cohen himself. He signed up to – indeed, co-authored – the Euston Manifesto, which explicitly noted that its supporters could campaign together for its main neo-conservative thrust while agreeing to differ... on the Iraq War!

So on Cohen's logic it was permissible for gentlemen of liberal breeding gathered in a pub to set aside their minor quibbles over the most devastating war of recent history in order to jointly promote their manifesto. But it was wrong to oppose that war alongside people who one might reasonably suspect harbour more conservative views on human sexuality.

The left-wing patina spread over this otherwise evidently-flawed posturing is supplied by the invocation of anti-fascism, with fascism extending to cover not just Saddam Hussein but the main organisations of British Muslims as well.

The inter-relationship of anti-fascism and anti-imperialism has become an emblematic source of confusion for those on the left who have moved towards an embrace of US power over the last twenty years. British academic and author Fred Halliday, who certainly was anti-imperialist for the early part of his career, announced in 1991 that given a choice between imperialism and fascism, he would embrace the former. As already argued, this is a false polarity. From the perspective of Halliday's affluent north London suburb of Muswell Hill, where the direct depredations of imperialism are felt lightly, and amount to no more than the replacement of a second-hand bookshop by a branch of Starbucks, that is a logical enough position. A British fascism's brute violence would threaten Halliday's way of life far more than British imperialism's incremental corruption does. But for much of the world, there is no choice – imperialism's domination in the Middle East is not occasionally but invariably accompanied by fascist-type methods of domination – indeed, as we have seen, European colonialism in the "Third World" has generally been more brutal than European fascism was, at least when the latter was imposed by a fascist regime on "its own" population. [34]

Cohen is a step further back than Halliday, however. He is in the tradition of a left which barely acknowledges the reality of the imperialist experience and its impact on world history at all, which buries its head in the sand regarding the crimes of colonialism and has absolutely no place for an understanding of imperialism in today's politics, even though the great majority of the world's people see it all too clearly. What Niall Ferguson and Andrew Roberts seek to justify – even exult in – Cohen and the other left neo-cons simply ignore. In both cases, their work helps prepare the way for a repetition of the crimes of Empire, and in neither case is this accidental.

This makes them accessories to the imperial historians' political crime in covering up most of the worst atrocities of the twentieth century. The practical consequence of this, beyond championing new wars of aggression, lies in denying the validity of any form of struggle or political experience beyond the range of the white metropolitan left and seeking to impose under cover of moral universalism the power of government's which are entirely beholden to big business.

The assumption that the Iraqi people could never achieve their own liberation from Saddam flows from this attitude. They were – Chalabi's fantasy guerillas aside – to be spectators at their own liberation by the beneficient US and British armies. The vast majority of secular Arab Iraqi democrats opposed to Saddam – the sort who spoke at numerous Stop the War rallies, but whom Cohen ignored because they did not fit his thesis – were against invasion as being the solution to the Baath dictatorship.

They knew history better than Cohen. Rightwing dictatorships were overthrown, or at any event displaced, in Spain, Greece, Portugal, Chile and South Africa. In all cases, external armed intervention played no part, and as a consequence democracy has sunk stable roots. The disaster in Iraq was the predictable – and by most of the left, predicted – outcome of the determination to substitute the power of US and British imperialism for solidarity with peoples fighting for their own liberation.

"Writers write badly when they have something to hide," Cohen noted. *What's Left* testified to the truth of that insight. Cohen has a lot to hide – the disaster of the war, occupation and its string of associated crimes from Abu Ghraib to Haditha. Even a bracing confession of error would not let him recover his bearings now. [35]

Last Hurrah

On the weekend in April 2006 that British troops were revealed as taking part in war games for a US-led attack on Iran and ten soldiers were wounded (one killed) in the military occupations of Afghanistan and Iraq, the same weekend that, coincidentally, tens of thousands of people turned out in Dublin to remember the "terrorists" of the 1916 rising, as they were dubbed by contemporary Labour and Liberal leaders, John Lloyd announced that the left in Britain must face a parting of the ways on the issue of imperialism or anti-imperialism.

The occasion for this sensational declaration was the publication of the Euston Manifesto, the product of a year of pub plotting – the document takes its name from the hostelry – by the leading lights of the pro-war punditry in Britain. It was the last intellectual throw by the pro-war left, who used their entrenched positions in the media and the blogosphere to create a furore about this, the appearance of a programme summarising their views on just where the rest of the left had gone wrong. [36]

In fact even at the outset, the Euston Manifesto was less a call to arms than a final instrument of surrender by the liberal warriors. This was made plain by the position it failed to assert – support for the Iraq War. On this even the pro-war left had, by 2006, to agree to differ. The embarrassed silence on this point was as clear a sign of the political collapse of the liberal shock-and-awe party as one could wish to see. If even the cream of pro-war punditry and academia could no longer agree to make the case for the Iraq War then that case was finally as dead as the proverbial Monty Python parrot. While the Eustonians could still make the case for "interventionism" in the abstract, they could no longer unite to defend it in its most dramatic particular.

And twenty people meeting in a central London pub was hardly the split trumpeted by Lloyd. In the Fourth International it may have been, as one or two of the Euston signatories doubtless recalled. But not in the left as a whole. Of course, the choice of licensed premises as the intellectual hothouse may have been a smart move in shaking off those fascist Muslims of their nightmares, but it has seldom been an insuperable barrier to attendance by prominent trade unionists, for example. None seem to have joined in, nevertheless.

The manifesto was intended by its progenitors to be a "new political alignment." Ambition considerably outstripped achievement in this respect. The Eustonians did not stand in elections, did not develop a membership base nor hold a democratic conference. They did not risk anything that might have allowed their political capacity to be measured, like organising a demonstration in support of their views. In fact The Euston Manifesto organisation did little or nothing over the next two years before calling it a day, declaring itself a "moment" rather than a "movement," although even that seems a mite generous.

The reason for its failure is that so much in the world today does indeed turn on the question Lloyd highlighted but the manifesto dared not address – imperialism and anti-imperialism. Imperialism is not just a matter of the Iraq War or even foreign policy as a whole, but something that touches on many aspects of domestic politics as well, from community cohesion to civil liberties to economic priorities.

This stubborn anti-anti-imperialism (pro-imperialism by way of a double negative of political positioning) led John Lloyd, without an apparent trace of self-awareness, to criticise the anti-war movement for allegedly forming "alliances with fundamentalist Islamic groups, whose policies on civil and human rights, including equal rights for women and gays, are deeply reactionary" while standing strong for his own pro-war alliance with George

Bush, whose policies on civil rights and equality for women and gays were ... what exactly? It is hardly surprising that this hypocrisy seems to some to be Islamophobic.

How the politics of anti-imperialism develop in a democratic and inclusive form, building on the real, actual unity of socialists, liberals, greens, trade unionists and democrats of all faiths and none achieved in the anti-war movement – that is a debate of consequence. But for those who portentously declaimed that "America is a great country" while having nothing to say on the "economic forms of equality," the best response was what actually happened – nothing.

Perhaps the authors had uneasily anticipated this denouement. Back in 2003, there was already an element of pathos in David Aaronovitch's contemplation of the anti-war movement. Even at the moment of greatest hubris, four days after the invasion began, he felt compelled to write: "Why has the anti-war movement in this country been so bloody big? Even last weekend's demonstrations, widely written off by sections of the press, struck me as being of an extraordinary size. And no, it is not obvious why such an unprecedented coalition should have come together now, and not at any other time in post-war history...it is by and large their kids, their fabulous teenagers, who are turning out for the spontaneous demos against the war. As they should. Far better being an active citizen than a moaning passive consumer of the latest mobile phone." [37]

The "cruise-missile liberals" not only lost the argument over Iraq. They lost their children too.

NOTES

Introduction

1 New Statesman, December 12 2005

Chapter One

1 The Guardian November 8 2001
2 Reinert, p 99; Dirks, p325-26; Brendon p 396
3 Bosworth p 375; Dirks pp. 27, 329
4 The Guardian January 27 2005
5 The Guardian July 23 2002
6 Wall Street Journal December 7 1992
7 Wall Street Journal January 8 1993
8 Wall Street Journal 21 January 1993
9 cited by Mirrlees in Mooers [ed] p 202
10 Wall Street Journal October 4 2001
11 Financial Times, October 2001
12 Daily Telegraph October 8 2001; Guardian October 10 2001
13 Independent report n.d
14 Reordering the World: the long-term implications of September 11, published by the FPC; Observer April 7 2002
15 Guardian 23 October 2003
16 Financial Times, 2004
17 New Statesman, 31 January 2005
18 Ferguson [2003], p.xvii; see Elkins pp10-12 for a sketch of Kenya's white settler community, in which Ferguson was raised.
19 Dirks, p 334; " a curiously old-fashioned sort of story-telling redolent of a bygone age of imperial historiography; the makers of history are 'great men' like Livingstone, Macaulay and, inevitably, Churchill" – see Mooers p. 118
20 Ferguson, [2003] p.367
21 Guardian October 31 2001

22 quoted in the review of Colossus by Martin Jacques in The Guardian June 5 2004

23 Daily Telegraph January 19 2005; Lal is a US academic who is one of the most outspoken advocates of a new imperialism and unambiguous about its nature – "Empires need to be distinguished from mere hegemony. Empires seek to control both the domestic and foreign policies of their allies, hegemony only their foreign policy." Empire should be used to secure the uncontrolled power of private property, against the threat from democracy on occasions, he argues – cited by Hanieh in Mooers [ed] pp 169, 172

24 cited by George Monbiot in The Guardian December 27 2005

25 Roberts, [2006], pp 7

26 cited by Johann Hari in The Independent, June 12 2006; Roberts, [1999], pp517-8

27 Daily Telegraph February 5 2005

28 Roberts, [2006], p.132

29 Guardian February 8 2003

30 The Guardian June 28 2006

31 Independent June 12 2005

32 Financial Times March 29 2007

33 James, p.629

34 The Independent June 7 2004

Chapter Two

1 BBC History Magazine, January 2008

2 cited by Robin Kelley in Cesaire, p.20

3 Cesaire, p.36; Mazower p. 587

4 Brendon, p 330; Porter [2004] p.63; Seymour, p. 64; Ferguson [2006] pp468-9

5 Brendon, pp 397-400

6 ibid p 360

7 Ferguson, [2006] p.343

8 Dutt, [1953], p.276; Johnson, Soundings no 37, p.86

9 A.E. Atmore in Eldridge, p. 118; Barnes, p.125

10 *Mazower pp 587-88*

11 *Bayly/Harper p 138*

12 *Brendon p 147*

13 *ibid pp 469, 396*

14 *Padmore, p.39*

15 *see Bayly/Harper p 25 for a discussion of this attitude in relation to Malaya*

16 *Jackson, p. 244; note also the view expressed by Christine Bolt in Eldridge, p. 142 that "racial and class prejudices were so intertwined in Victorian times that it is hard to separate them"*

17 *Brendon, p. 118*

18 *Davis [2002] pp23-59; Dutt, [1947], p 106; Brendon p 231*

19 *Tsiang, p.43*

20 *Davis; Biel, p.16; Moore in Eldridge, p 80; railways seem to play a particular role in excusing the inexcusable – witness the oft-repeated boast that Mussolini at least "made the trains run on time." This, too, is a myth – Italian railways remained chaotic throughout the fascist dictatorship and only improved in the post-war era, see Bosworth p. 439*

21 *Dutt, [1947], p 217*

22 *Misra, p. 215; Brendon, pp 397-400*

23 *Ferguson [2006] p. 414*

24 *New Statesman June 26 2006)*

25 *Marx, [1847/1975], p112*

26 *cited by George Monbiot in The Guardian 27 December 2005*

27 *Dirks, p.151*

28 *Randeep Ramesh in The Guardian, November 18 2002; Ferguson, [2003], p.216*

29 *Dirks p.145-47*

30 *Davis cited by Chalmers Johnson in Soundings, p.86, Misra p.92*

31 *Frieden, p 397; Bayly/Harper p 378; Epstein pp8-9*

32 *Barnes, pp. 152-55; Campbell p.99*

33 *Rodney p 171-72, 22; Campbell p 99*

34 *Hyam, p 18*

35 *Falola p 27-28*

36 Padmore, pp 51, 80

37 Padmore p 45 and p 104 for examples; Goering quote from http://en.thinkexist.com/quotation/education_is_dangerous-every_educated_person_is_a/155972.html

38 cited in Bricmont, p 42

39 Brendon p 13; see Dalrymple p. 432 for a discussion of the legal position in 1857 India

40 Dalrymple, p. 315

41 Brendon p 133; Dalrymple, p.364

42 Dalrymple p 454; Seymour p. 29

43 Brendon p 138

44 Hyam p 35

45 Misra, p. 194; League Against Imperialism; Bayly/Harper, pp18, 78; Brendon p 391

46 Padmore, pp 228, 93

47 Barnes, p169

48 Hyam, p 262

49 Elkins, p xiv

50 ibid p 366

51 Padmore, p 60

52 Judd p 351

53 David Anderson The Guardian December 1 1999

54 Brendon p 554; Seumas Milne in The Guardian January 27 2005

55 Brendon p 560-61

56 Bayly/Harper pp 305, 409

57 ibid p 524

58 Curtis, [2003], p. 341-2; Bayly/Harper p 449-56; p 483

59 Newsinger p 208; Bayly/Harper p 453, 481

60 Perry Anderson in London Review of Books April 24 2008

61 ibid, cites Robert Holland's Britain and the Revolt in Cyprus 1954-59 which Anderson describes as "perhaps the best single study in the historiography of decolonisation

62 Brendon p 505; Seumas Milne in Guardian January 27, 2005

63 Newsinger, p 138; Bayly/Harper p 441

64 Brendon pp200, 237; Darcy cited in Padmore p 72
65 Bricmont, p 29
66 Brendon p 221
67 Dalrymple p 425
68 Brendon p 122
69 Padmore, p 102
70 Brendon p 234
71 Porter [2004] p 233; Porter [1975] p. 130 ff; Feuchtwanger, p 229
72 Porter [2004] p. 288
73 Cole, p 527
74 Porter[2004], p.293
75 Porter [2004] p 206; Kiernan, [1972], p. 81
76 Brendon pp 360, 369, 385
77 Porter [2004] p.189; Reinert p. 213
78 The Guardian July 11 2006; quote from The Wars of the World, cited by
Gopal in The Guardian June 28 2006
79 Curtis [2004] pp 310-317
80 see Newsinger
81 Bayly/Harper p 550
82 Daily Mail, January 15 2005
83 Cole, Policy Futures in Education, vol. 2, nos 3-4, 2004 p.529
84 Hochschild, p232-3; see also Ascherson
85 Frieden, p 80
86 Brendon p 353
87 ibid p 365
88 Porter[2004], p 166
89 Stoecker (ed), pp 47-64
90 Kiernan [1972] p 237
91 Hyam p 44; RIIA [1937] and [1938]; Cain/Hopkins 2 p 228; Barnes;
inter alia
92 Naima Bouteldja and Stuart Hodkinson in The Guardian 17 May 2006;
Mazower p 592; Lieven in Financial Times 21 August 2007; see also
House/MacMaster, pp33-60
93 Bayly/Harper p 149

94 ibid pp 180-181
95 Bosworth pp 50, 375, 381-84
96 Time Magazine, May 5 1947

Chapter Three

1 http://www.guardian.co.uk/politics/2006/mar/21/iraq.iraq1
2 Kampfner p 4
3 Dalrymple, p 441
4 cited by Philip Stephens, Financial Times, April 11 2008
5 ISP/NSC Briefing Paper 05/01
6 Ali[2002] p 208
7 Aburish [2005], p. 21
8 Hyam, p 54
9 Hyam, p. 50; Abrahams (ed) p 10; Campbell p 73
10 Sluglett and Farouk-Sluglett p 2
11 Hourani p 330
12 Ferguson, [2006], p. 412; Mooers (ed) p. 129; Salucci pp 127-8
13 Brendon p 320
14 Sluglett, pp 32-33
15 Yergin, p.393
16 Brendon p 168
17 Hyam p 191
18 Ali [2002], p. 97
19 Keddie, p 76; Engdahl, p.93
20 Keddie, pp 3, 188
21 see Kapuscinski, particularly chapter two on the Shah's regime
22 see Hanna Batatu's magisterial work on Iraq's 20th century history until the early 1970s, and in particular his analysis of its social structure and the development of both the Communist and Baath parties
23 Brendon p 111
24 Amin in "Political Islam in the service of Imperialism"
25 Rashid p 130
26 Independent, October 15 1998

27 *Engdahl, pp 253-4*
28 *Financial Times, October 16 2008*
29 *IWMD, p.17*
30 *see Murray/German inter alia*
31 *The controversy over Iraqi casualty numbers since the invasion of 2003 is endless. It arises because no-one amongst the occupying powers thought it worth keeping count. Robust demographical research puts the figure of excess civilian deaths (not necessarily all directly a result of violence) at around one million. The Iraqi government has itself acknowledged over 150,000 violent deaths, the lowest serious estimate.*
32 *Engdahl, p 258*
33 *ibid, p 263*
34 *Spokesman, p 11*
35 *Boal cited by Mooers, in Mooers (ed) p 4*
36 *Hanieh in Mooers (ed) p 167; Chandrasekaran, pp.322, 68*

Chapter Four

1 *cited in Kiernan, [1972], p 24*
2 *see Murray/German p237ff for an examination of this*
3 *George, p 31*
4 *Jenkins, pp 500-1*
5 *Dutt [1953], p.277*
6 *Kiernan [1972] p xxx*
7 *ibid p 280*
8 *Dutt [1953] p.319*
9 *Owen in Brown/Louis (eds), p 191*
10 *cited in Clough, p 40*
11 *Dutt, [1953] p 321*
12 *Davis [2002] p 165*
13 *British Socialist Party 1st annual conference report, 1912, p.21; for more on the SDF anti-imperialist tradition see John Foster speech in 1984, in MML Bulletin Autumn 1984, p.3*
14 *Dutt [1953] p. 322; Newsinger, p.146*

15 *Challinor, p 21; Tsiang p. 95; Judd p. 209*
16 *Dutt [1953] p 323*
17 *Clough, p 42*
18 *Gupta, p 305; Bayly/Harper p. 96*
19 *Gupta, p 326*
20 *Labour Party, Labour's Colonial Policy, The Plural Society, 1956 p 10*
21 *Gupta, p 336*
22 *Cain/Hopkins 2, p 178*
23 *http://www.number10.gov.uk/Page1297*
24 *Porteous, pp 123, 140*
25 *Time, December 10 2001*

Chapter Five

1 *see Seymour's Liberal Defence of Murder for a survey of the evolution of liberal imperialism worldwide*
2 *The Observer, December 28 2003; Hitchens, p 54*
3 *Pentagon press release; The Guardian April 29 2003*
4 *Private Eye, n.d.; Hitchens p 8*
5 *The Guardian, April 1 2003*
6 *The Observer, March 23 2003; Hitchens, p. 67*
7 *Lloyd, pp 3, 9-10, 13*
8 *New Statesman, April 14 2003*
9 *Lloyd p 17*
10 *Hitchens, p 18*
11 *ibid p 47*
12 *ibid p 73*
13 *ibid p 13*
14 *ibid pp 83,101*
15 *Seymour p 19*
16 *Lloyd p 16; The Observer, August 3 2003*
17 *Hitchens, p 42. Since the fiasco of his wartime punditry, Hitchens has, Dorian Gray-like, deteriorated. He has increasingly come to rely on a mixture of personal abuse and Martini machismo in dealing with his critics. He*

publicly described US country-rock band the Dixie Chicks as "fucking fat slags" for criticising President Bush. The following are from his review of Michael Moore's Fahrenheit 9/11 on Slate.msn.com, posted June 21 2004: "I never quite know whether Moore is as ignorant as he looks, or even if that would be humanly possible." And, urging the director to join him in a debate: "Any time, Michael my boy...Any show. Any place. Any platform. Let's see what you're made of."

18 Kamm, p 19

19 ibid p 36

20 ibid p 16

21 Roberts, [2006] p 265

22 Kamm p 114

23 ibid p 115

24 New Statesman, May 5 2003; Seymour p 11

25 see New Statesman April 7 2003

26 New Statesman, October 29 2001

27 New Statesman, October 29 2001

28 For Miller's record see inter alia Woman of Mass Derision, The Guaridan Weekend, March 11 2006

29 The Observer, July 13 2003

30 Seymour p 11

31 Cited by Andrew Murray in the Morning Star, August 11 2003; The Observer February 16 2003

32 Cohen, p 146

33 Independent, September 23 2004

34 Seymour p 187

35 Cohen, p 96

36 http://www.guardian.co.uk/commentisfree/2006/apr/14/lloydpiece

37 The Guardian March 25 2003

Bibliography

Abdullah, Thabit	*Dictatorship, Imperialism and Chaos,* London: 2006
Abrahams, Eddie (ed)	*The New Warlords,* London: 1994
Aburish, Said K.	*The Rise, Corruption and Coming Fall of the House of Saud* London: 1994
Ali, Tariq	*The Clash of Fundamentalisms,* London: 2002
Amin, Samir	*Political Islam in the Service of Imperialism,* essay 2007
	Obsolescent Capitalism, London: 2003
	Empire of Chaos, New York: 1992
Anderson, David	*Histories of the Hanged, London*: 2005
Anderson, Perry	*The Divisions of Cyprus* in London Review of Books 24 April 2008
Ascherson, Neal	*The King Incorporated,* London: 1999 (1963)
Baker, Bill	*The Social Democratic Federation and the Boer War,* London: 1974
Barnes, Leonard	*Empire or Democracy?,* London: 1939
Batatu, Hanna	*The Old Social Classes and the Revolutionary Movements of Iraq,* London: 2004 (1978)
Baumgart, Winifred	*Imperialism,* Oxford: 1982
Bayly, Christopher & Harper, Tim	*Forgotten Wars: the End of Britain's Asian Empire,* London: 2007
Biel, Robert	*The New Imperialism,* London: 2000
Birch, Lionel	*The Demand for Colonies;* London: n.d. (1935?)
Bosworth, R.J.B.	*Mussolini's Italy,* London: 2006
Bremer, Paul	*My Year in Iraq,* New York: 2006
Brendon, Piers	*The Decline and Fall of the British Empire 1781-1997* London: 2007
Bricmont, Jean	*Humanitarian Imperialism,* New York: 2006
British Socialist Party	*1st Annual Conference: Official Report* London:1912
Brown, Judith M & Louis, Wm. Roger (eds)	*The Oxford History of the British Empire: The Twentieth Century* Oxford: 1999
Cain, P.J. & Hopkins, A.G.	*British Imperialism 1: Innovation & Expansion 1688-1914*
	British Imperialism 2: Crisis & Deconstruction 1914-1990 Harlow: 1993
Campbell, Alexander	*It's Your Empire, London:* 1945
Cesaire, Aime	*Discourse on Colonialism,* New York: 2000 (1955)
Catherwood, Christopher	*Churchill's Folly* New York: 2004

Challinor, Raymond	*The Origins of British Bolshevism*, London:1997
Chandrasekaran, Rajiv	*Imperial Life in the Emerald City*, London: 2007
Clarke, Richard	*Against All Enemies*, London:2004
Clough, Robert	*Labour: A Party Fit for Imperialism*, London: 1992
Cohen, Nick	*What's Left? How Liberals Lost their Way*, London: 2007
Cole, Mike	*Rule Britannia' and the New American Empire* in Policy Futures in Education, vol. 2 nos 3 & 4, 2004
Cooper, Robert	*The Breaking of Nations*, London: 2003
Curtis, Mark	*Web of Deceit*, London 2003
Dalrymple, William	*The Last Mughal*, London: 2006
Davis, Mike	*Late Victorian Holocausts*, London: 2002
Dirks, Nicholas B.	*The Scandal of Empire*, Cambridge (USA): 2006
Dreyfuss, Robert	*Devil's Game*, New York: 2005
Dutt, R. Palme	*India Today*, Bombay: 1947 (1940)
	The Crisis of Britain and the British Empire, London: 1953
Eldridge, C.C. (ed)	*British Imperialism in the 19th Century*, London 1984
Elkins, Caroline	*Britain's Gulag*, London: 2005
Engdahl, William	*A Century of War*, London: 1992
Epstein, Israel	*From Opium War to Liberation*, Peking: 1956
Falola, Toyin (ed)	*Britain and Nigeria: Exploitation or Development?* London: 1987
Farouk-Sluglett, Marion & Sluglett, Peter	*Iraq since 1958: from Revolution to Dictatorship*, London: 2003 (1987)
Ferguson, Niall	*Empire: How Britain Made the Modern World*, London: 2003
	Colossus: The Rise and Fall of the American Empire, London: 2005
	The Wars of the World, London: 2006
Feuchtwanger, E.J.	*Democracy and Empire*: Britain 1865-1914, London: 1986
Fisk, Robert	*The Great War for Civilisation* London: 2005
Frieden, Jeffrey R.	*Global Capitalism: Its Fall and Rise in the Twentieth Century*, New York: 2006
George, Susan	Hijacking America, Cambridge: 2008
Gupta, Partha	Imperialism and the British Labour Movement, London: 1975
Halliday, Fred	Two Hours that Shook the World, London: 2002
Hitchens, Christopher	*Regime Change*, London: 2003
Hochschild, Adam	*King Leopold's Ghost*, London: 1999
Hourani, Albert	*A History of the Arab Peoples*, London: 2005 (1991)

House, Jim & MacMaster, Neil   *Paris 1961*, Oxford: 2006

Hughes, Solomon   *War on Terror Inc*, London: 2007

Hyam, Ronald   *Britain's Declining Empire*, Cambridge: 2006

Jackson, T.A.   *Ireland Her Own*, London: 1976 (1947)

James, Lawrence   *The Rise and Fall of the British Empire*, London: 1994

Jenkins, Roy   *Gladstone* London: 2002 (1995)

Johnson, Chalmers   *The Sorrows of Empire*, London: 2004

   The Good Empire in Soundings, Winter 2007

Judd, Denis   *Empire*, London: 1996

Kagan, Robert   *Paradise & Power, London:* 2003

Kamm, Oliver   *Anti-Totalitarianism*, London: 2005

Kapuscinski, Ryszard   *Shah of Shahs*, London: 2006 (1985)

Keddie, Nikki R.   *Modern Iran*, New Haven: 2003

Kiernan, Victor   *The Lords of Human Kind, Harmondsworth:* 1972

   America, the New Imperialism London: 2005 [1978]

Klare, Michael   *Blood and Oil, London: 2004*

League Against Imperialism   *The British Empire, London:* n.d. (1936?)

Lloyd, John   *Iraq and World Order, London:* 2003

Losev, Sergei & Tyssovsky, Yuri   *The Middle East: Oil and Policy, Moscow: 1980*

MacKenzie, John M.   *Propaganda and Empire, Manchester:* 1984

Mandani, Mahmoud   *Good Muslim, Bad Muslim New York:* 2004

Marx, Karl   *The Poverty of Philosophy, Moscow 1975 (1847)*

Mazower, Mark   *Hitler's Empire: Nazi Rule in Occupied Europe,*

   London: 2008

Misra, Maria   *Vishnu's Crowded Temple, London: 2007*

Mooers, Colin (ed)   *The New Imperialists: Ideologies of Empire*, Oxford: 2006

Murray, Andrew   *Flashpoint: World War III*, London/Chicago: 1997
Murray, Andrew &   Stop the War, London: 2005
German, Lindsey

Newsinger, John   *The Blood Never Dried: A People's History of the British Empire*,
   London: 2006

Padmore, George   *Africa: Britain's Third Empire*, London: 1949

Porteous, Tom   *Britain in Africa*, London: 2008

Porter, Bernard   *The Lion's Share*, Harlow: 1975

   The Absent-Minded Imperialists, Oxford: 2004

Prashad, Vijay	*The Darker Nations*, New York: 2007
Rashid, Ahmed	*Taliban*, London: 2000
Research Unit for Political Economy	*Behind the Invasion of Iraq*, New York: 2003
Roberts, Andrew	*Salisbury: Victorian Titan*, London: 1999
--	*A History of the English-Speaking Peoples Since 1900*, London: 2006
Rodney, Walter	*How Europe Under-Developed Africa*, Washington: 1981 (1972)
Royal Institute for Affairs	*The Colonial Problem*, London: 1937 International *Germany's Claim for Colonies*, London: 1938
Salucci, Ilario	*A People's History of Iraq*, Chicago: 2005
Seymour, Richard	*The Liberal Defence of Murder*, London: 2008
Stoecker, Helmuth (ed)	*German Imperialism in Africa*, London: 1986
Sturmer, Michael	*The German Empire*, London: 2000
Tsiang, Tingfu F.	*Labour and Empire*, New York: 1923
Verulam, Frank	*Imperialism and the People*, London: n.d. (1944?)
Yergin, Daniel	*The Prize*

Index